BLACK BELL

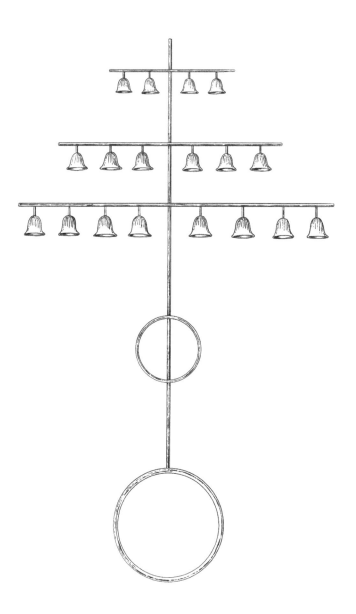

BLACK BELL

ALISON C. ROLLINS

COPPER CANYON PRESS

PORT TOWNSEND, WASHINGTON

Cover art: From Moses Roper's *A Narrative of the Adventures and Escape of Moses Roper, from American Slavery,* 1837. Courtesy of Documenting the American South, Libraries of the University of North Carolina, Chapel Hill. Reillustration by Jonathan Leyton.

Copper Canyon Press is in residence at Fort Worden State Park in Port Townsend, Washington, under the auspices of Centrum. Centrum is a gathering place for artists and creative thinkers from around the world, students of all ages and backgrounds, and audiences seeking extraordinary cultural enrichment.

LIBRARY OF CONGRESS CATALOGING-IN-PUBLICATION DATA
Names: Rollins, Alison C., author.
Title: Black bell / Alison C. Rollins ; a collection of poems by Alison C. Rollins.
Description: Port Townsend, Washington : Copper Canyon Press, 2024.
Identifiers: LCCN 2023049138 (print) | LCCN 2023049139 (ebook) |
ISBN 9781556597008 (paperback) | ISBN 9781619322943 (epub)
Subjects: LCGFT: Poetry.
Classification: LCC PS3618.O549 B56 2024 (print) |
LCC PS3618.O549 (ebook) | DDC 811/.6—dc23/eng/20231019
LC record available at https://lccn.loc.gov/2023049138
LC ebook record available at https://lccn.loc.gov/2023049139

9 8 7 6 5 4 3 2 FIRST PRINTING

COPPER CANYON PRESS
Post Office Box 271
Port Townsend, Washington 98368
www.coppercanyonpress.org

ALSO BY ALISON C. ROLLINS

Library of Small Catastrophes

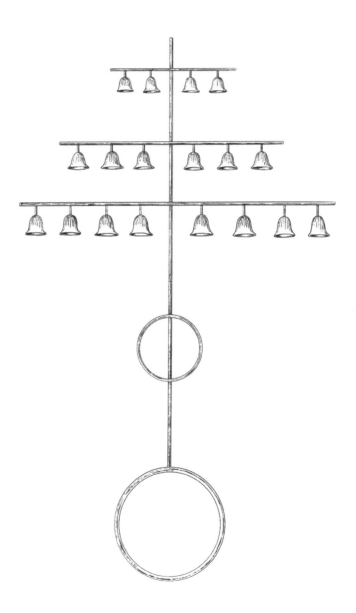

Another mode of punishment which this man adopted, was that of using iron horns, with bells, attached to the back of the slave's neck. . . . This instrument he used to prevent the negroes running away, being a very ponderous machine, several feet in height, and the cross pieces being two feet four, and six feet in length. This custom is generally adopted among the slave-holders in South Carolina, and some other slave States. One morning, about an hour before day break, I was going on an errand for my master; having proceeded about a quarter of a mile, I came up to a man . . . who had caught a young girl that had run away with the above machine on her. She had proceeded four miles from her station.

MOSES ROPER, *A Narrative of the Adventures and Escape of Moses Roper, from American Slavery* (1837)

The moment we choose to love we begin to move towards freedom, to act in ways that liberate ourselves and others.

BELL HOOKS, *Outlaw Culture: Resisting Representations*

The clanging in her head, begun as a churchbell heard from a distance, was by then a tight cap of pealing bells around her ears.

TONI MORRISON, *Beloved*

When I wrote something that finally had it, I would say it aloud and it would come alive, become real. It would start repeating itself and I'd know, that's struck, that's true. Like a bell.

AUDRE LORDE, *Sister Outsider*

CONTENTS

I

xi

BLACK BELL

I

Love and life

Interested me so

That I dared to knock

At the door of the cosmos

SUN RA, "Door of the Cosmos"

A Bell Is a Messenger of Time

*To be performed with bells on. All "reading" is performance,
some performance is "reading."*

The neck's
heavy load
is light-headed.
The single sound,
everywhere at once.
Black bell, black bell,
have you any cool?
May all enemies be this ridiculous!
You put a face to the name of my noise.
The sum of a shadow, invisible to whom?
Can't you hear me comin'? A pyramid
of bells singin' from tween my ears.
That's why when you speak of me, my ears ring,
ring with the melody of a thousand tambourines.
To get ahead of myself, I got freedom off my chest.
I'm a woman in the company of bells. Am I their company? Are they mine?
No one seems to have a handle on the hex, aside from the tattletale town crier.
You looked at me the wrong way. I was moved, surrounded on all sides by bells.
Barnacle bells. Irremovable attachments. Even when I ghost you, you still hear me, still
hear me fixin' to arrive, a jingle of labor from on high. The sound takes a toll on the body.
The crops respond well to sound waves. You hear the river before you see it. Ever-present
eavesdropper. A bell is a messenger of time. Don't kill the messenger; make a killing with
the message. Forgive-me-not. The bells run interference. Ring in remove. The bells, placed
head over heels. The mind (left in the dark), in the thicket, where all the clocks have stopped.
When all the clocks stopped, I laid my burden down. Hearing, the last sense to escape the
body.*

A WOMAN WITH IRON HORNS AND BELLS ON, TO KEEP HER FROM RUNNING AWAY.

Black Bell

A bell's dome represents the whole universe, the flat bottom represents the earth, and the hollow inside represents the space between the rest of the universe and the earth. When you strike a bell it sends a message from Earth out into the universe. Before reading, strike a bell tuned to F, the note connected to the heart chakra.

Sound can give things a color,
the way eyes can smile.

To give yourself back to yourself,
you must increasingly fold inward
at the etched creases of your palms.

To turn black is to join the fold.
To turn back is to face the music
of the shotgun's open mouth.

We watch to see
how black bell's holding up.
By a thread? A string? A hook? A rope?

She sleeps a sleep of the sleepless—
a bell's body is never at rest.

The Respiratory System

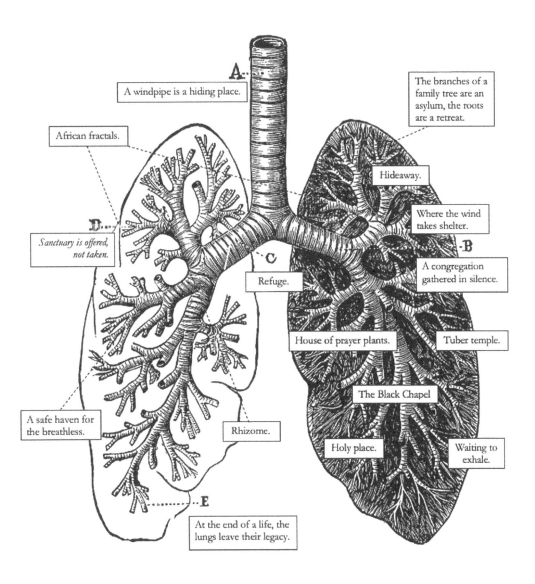

A windipe is a hiding place.

The branches of a family tree are an asylum, the roots are a retreat.

African fractals.

Hideaway.

Where the wind takes shelter.

Sanctuary is offered, not taken.

A congregation gathered in silence.

Refuge.

House of prayer plants.

Tuber temple.

The Black Chapel

A safe haven for the breathless.

Rhizome.

Holy place.

Waiting to exhale.

At the end of a life, the lungs leave their legacy.

Phillis Wheatley Takes Turing Test

Italicized text should be spoken via a computer-generated or synthetic voice. Unitalicized text should be read aloud by a human.

🔊 *We will begin now if you are ready.*

> I was born awake.

🔊 *Are you game?*

> No, but I can tell
> you are a boar.

🔊 *What is your name?*

> I am not subject
> to definition, or any
> sound you might make
> to beckon me.

🔊 *How is the weather?*

> It is hard to breathe today.
> Air, as unnoticed as necessary,
> often has its way with me.

🔊 *Are you a man?*

> A man is an unruly horse
> housed in a tortoise shell.
> I am no more a man than
> smoke is a signal of war.

🔊 *Are you white?*

> Whatever supremacy
> governs this moment
> is the tool by which
> we color our threat.

🔊 *How old are you?*

> As old as any number
> divisible by conquest.

🔊 *Whom do you answer to?*

> Love.

🔊 *Are you Christian?*

> Neither height nor depth,
> nor any other creature,
> shall be able to separate
> us from the love of god.

🔊 *So you are a believer?*

> Faith is an ocean of rage
> at rest, a merciful calm
> that thumps in my chest.

🔊 *Where are you from?*

> A darling collection of cells
> blood-dazzled with sunrays.
> From two beings welded in delight,
> from the lull of lullabies
> earth hums to split open.

🔊 *Where do you call home?*

> My body—the mirage
> of a wooden bowl with
> water held in its mouth.

🔊 *What do you do?*

> I arrange my hands
> into birds that sing
> songs only I know.

🔊 *I meant what is your occupation?*

> To evade. To make a living
> by staying alive.

🔊 *Are you free?*

       Tomorrow I was.

🔊 *Are you out of your mind?*

       Near my head is nothing
       but distances, walking toward
       the shadow of truth.

🔊 *Do you know Latin?*

       Lung comes from the Latin *levis* or "light,"
       the Old High German *lungun*
       or literally "the light organ,"
       so called perhaps because
       in a cook's pot the lungs of an animal float
       while the liver and heart do not.

🔊 *What do you fear?*

       Both the limits and limitlessness of
       your imagination.

🔊 *Are you an early bird or a night owl?*

       Either way, I am hidden in plain sight.

🔊 *What does a normal day look like for you?*

unstressed   unstressed   stressed
stressed   stressed
stressed   unstressed
unstressed   stressed
stressed   unstressed   unstressed

🔊 *Do you know a good joke?*

Something funny is afoot
that isn't funny at all.

🔊 *Can you write poetry?*

Even golden-haired trees
are lyric in the fall, the bees
sound off with elegies
for Emmett, soliloquies
of dewy insects, little dizzies
offer their odes. We till
the earth with the departed's
name. Until. Until. Until . . .

🔊 *Are you real?*

As real as time, as the border
of one country from another,
as the poison in Socrates's cup,
as every toy's right to break.

🔊 *Have you only told the truth?*

       I know what I have said.
       I do not know what you have heard.

Riding with Death

after Jean-Michel Basquiat

A single white horse
sounds the skeleton key

that opens the door of
music. For the repass,

I—the caregiver—ride in,
barrelhead, empty-handed.

To "take care of" means
both caretaking and killing.

My mother took care of
my grandmother. No.

My mother smothered
my grandmother,

meaning acted as her caregiver
until she passed away.

By then, my mother was
already dead, slain by
her mother in youth.

You may wonder,
then, how I came to be.

Love, this poem has already
taken care of the explanation.

Picture me in the form
of a skeletal white horse,
gallivanting, galloping
out of the sea.

My hair spray—a salted wetness
to hold the unruly in place.

My ancestors are gone.
Gone with the wind. Fabulous.
Air filled with critical fabulations.

Foam. Spindrift speaks of
unforeseeable conditions.

When I think about violence
or my progenitors,
my memory topples, tumbles.

The Loophole of Retreat, or The Love below, as Above

for Harriet Jacobs

I
see you,
peeping Tom,
beside yourself with
rage at what I done did,
hands gone idle from deprivation.
I see you, Uncle, with your fingers at the
trapdoor, to place crumbs of a biscuit to my mouth
in the dark. Through a hole the size of a mustard seed,
I affix my eye and become faith itself, become the all-seeing
god in female form, the grown-woman grammar of Black vernacular.
Congregating mice enter my sanctuary, sniffing, praying with their teeth.
There go the train of my soul, dragging on the ground like a wedding gown.
The gravity of a grandmother's black hole. Being, both bound and intergalactic.
I, the wholeness of erasure, an invisible
matter hiding in an attic of entrapment.
Red ants eat through my legs, freedom
tiptoes on acid rain. Master don't know
where I be. Unbecoming. I be winded
in a window gone South. Up North, I
levitate on trip wire, limbs suspended
in dank air, indecent ligaments, numb
accomplices. Desensitized. Hair matted.
Nails gnarled. I swallow the steely dust,
my alchemist lips bleed metallic, a sweet
tune to the touch of a broken tongue.
Hear my children singing from below?
Come closer! Let Momma smell you
through the walls, let Momma's silence softly break.
This is what it means to watch over. This is what it feels like to hold your own.

Space Is the Place

The stars, so eager to be spent,
burned a hole in my pocket.

My plan was to take them
to show my grandmother.

But which way is home from death?
Sail away with me to a dreamscape

that sleeps at the top of the mountain
only beauty knows how to climb.

With your carabiner ears attached
at my childbearing hips,

I'm more aware of what I'm not
than what I am.

Lack made itself at home in my navel.
Well, I'll be damned what can come

from damnation. Constraint makes
possible a kind of freedom.

A pigeonhole—my way into heaven.
A fox-trot—my way back out.

Performance Directions

Remove the pages of the poem "Hymn of Inscape" from throughout the book.

Notice that the poem is composed of quatrains, or four-line stanzas, as well as several visuals. Cut each of the stanzas into its own small box, to get forty-eight total boxes. Cut each of the visuals into its own small box, to get twelve visuals. You should now have sixty total boxes of paper.

Next, you will need sixty miniature envelopes, as well as sixty postage stamps. On the front of each envelope, write a different emotion from the List of Feelings on the following page. Additionally, in the top-right corner of each envelope, affix a postage stamp.

Look through your sixty pieces of paper and choose a stanza or visual to be placed in an envelope according to how the text or image makes you feel. Do not worry if the two are not a "perfect match." You must, however, ensure that each piece of paper is placed into its own individual envelope.

Once you have completed this, wait for further instruction.

LIST OF FEELINGS

1. loving
2. fearful
3. rejected
4. amused
5. stressed
6. enraged
7. lonely
8. lost
9. resentful
10. surprised
11. ambivalent
12. frustrated
13. irritated
14. happy
15. bitter
16. disgusted
17. excited
18. pleasured
19. joyful
20. pained

21. hopeful
22. jealous
23. doubtful
24. ashamed
25. sad
26. embarrassed
27. ecstatic
28. alienated
29. eager
30. guilty
31. distrusting
32. confused
33. abhorrent
34. petty
35. worried
36. tired
37. fatigued
38. proud
39. anxious
40. satisfied

41. nervous
42. vengeful
43. disoriented
44. regretful
45. troubled
46. grieving
47. angry
48. bored
49. malaise
50. afraid
51. apprehensive
52. disappointed
53. annoyed
54. mad
55. inspired
56. creative
57. distraught
58. overwhelmed
59. moved
60. touched

Hymn of Inscape

We build our temples for tomorrow, strong as we know how, and we stand on top of the mountain, free within ourselves.

LANGSTON HUGHES, "The Negro Artist and the Racial Mountain"

I. A BOX DIAGRAM

II. A BLACK BODY

In linguistics, box diagrams
or cubes make use of a shape
or area in their construction.
A light-headed box is empty.

A decision tree is a Black family,
bodies planted right side up.
A box is made in the image of
its maker's mountain.

If life in a box is a pretty life,
was Henry "Box" Brown
pretty? Does a pretty boy
make a handsome man?

A poem is built like a box,
each stanza a four-cornered
room. Throbbing temples
make headway for freedom.

With a heavy heart, a hard head
makes a soft behind. Malcolm
X was imprisoned in a box [X] of
metal [not mental] bars.

Instructions are included for
folding cardboard or
nailing wood slats into
a home away from home.

Brick by brick, box by box,
we construct the architecture of
tomorrow from today.
Past is just blue's blueprint.

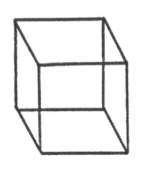

III. A HANDSOME MAN

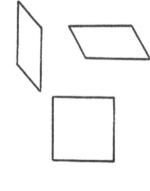

IV. PRETTY BOYS

Airy. Dark. Treasured.
Once upon a time, I learned
I was lonely but not alone.
Then, loneliness let loose.

The doctor describes it as
a "species of mental alienation."
Colors run. Colors bleed.
My mind, a porous plantation.

In *Life in a Box Is a Pretty Life*,
Dawn Lundy Martin poses
a question: *Where is my house?*
But it is not Dawn Lundy Martin,

it is the poem's speaker [beatbox]
who asks of themself,
What to know of the body's refusal to open,
of its hidden cave?

Implanted in the breast of
every man is a stolen
chest. In the chambers of
man's heart is a hum.

Dr. Samuel A. Cartwright
discovered *Drapetomania*,
"the disease causing slaves
to run away."

I first heard Monica Youn
read her poem "Detail of the
Rice Chest" in Sewanee, TN.
The poem contains the line:

I made [X] inscrutable.
I put [X] into the box.
Readers love a reveal,
a POP goes the weasel!

The Presence of the Body

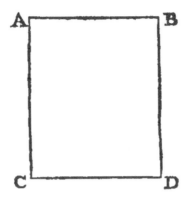

To Pronounce Me Dead

Dead upon arrival. Say: *dad*.
Call me: *daddy,* or *zaddy*
if you're nasty. Born bad:
the hereafter is child's play.
I single-parent my petulance.
Water under the breasts
refers to a past life.
Here and now, I am
a homebody. This land
made for you and me,
or you and you alone.
Wind, begone. Trees begotten.
Even though the space
between us is evergreen,
do still try to keep in touch.

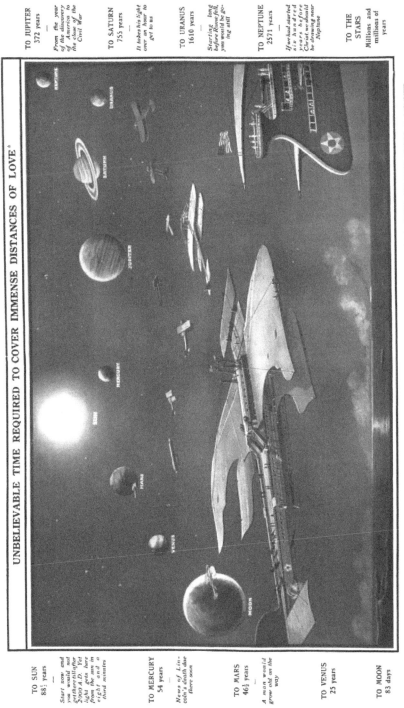

UNBELIEVABLE TIME REQUIRED TO COVER IMMENSE DISTANCES OF LOVE*

IF MAN SHOULD INVADE SPACE.—A RACE FOR SUN, MOON, AND PLANETS AT THE TERRIFIC SPEED OF TWO MILES A MINUTE

*I don't care about your past
I just want our love to last*

JAMES BROWN, "Cold Sweat"

Love in Outer Space

Because the bee
in my bonnet
is the B in my bed,
who I can't and I
won't stop bumping,
we do the humpty
hump. My big nose
nestled in her sassafras.
At attention, we round
each other out. At ease,
her peach is a galaxy.

Now and later is a square
I quietly hold on my tongue,
my mouth an empty gesture.
Spaced out between her legs,
I am an astronaut.
The gravity of my offense
adds up to a rational number.

When the heavens are free
from light, I sit desire on my lap.
She is stardust, and I,
as it were, am impossible.
When she asks for space,
she is the future. When she
asks for a room, it is the end.
I place before her chutes,
ladders, and whatever else
might fall from the sky.

[American Journal]

after Robert Hayden

here among them   the americans   you know what it is
what it was   what it will be   the stalks of their purple
throats like lilacs   their sounds reckless as mercy
how best to describe these beings   born alien
homeless everywhere   unafraid to die

the meek   do inherit   the earth   only after the new
world becomes the old country   with no pot to piss in
nor window to throw it out of   the children strike me
as angels of bread   latchkey kids who sell pig snoots
and loose squares to space travelers such as myself

charming savages   first world problems   these are
the ones left behind   the others bound long ago for
jupiter and neptune   helmets polished like new cars
bodies covered in papier-mâché   some can still recall
the white puffy suits   how hard the fabric was to sew

under disguise   i easily pass for an american
wool pulled over my scalp   the color of day's end
drooped across my shoulders   i know their signals
for love and anger   their etiquette for how to survive
their customhouse when fear comes to roost

i trace the great migration   follow the trail to detroit
gawk at the lions carved from stone   their stoic majesty
slippery as catfish   the air cries tear gas   grief   driven
out by water   although they want it in the worst way
the clouds no longer hand out rain

on the south side of chicago   i   watch   a man   jump off
a hospital roof   i record the way his gown inflates
his body a hot-air balloon   fact and fantasy never twice
the same   i make a note   the people could fly   they leave
go north of the future

in new york i observe the women   the last of the american
dream   i was told they can still grow a body   mystical
how they bleed and do not die   birds-of-paradise sprout
from their tulips   they call them the underground astronauts
their breasts hang   a prepackaged food supply

worshippers of waste   the americans recycle the past
they swim in plastic bags up to their necks
build machines to make their lives better
then grow fearful of what they have created
technology merely their mirror

the reflection of their own fragile image
these people are grandfathered in to history
history now obsolete   to lie means to tell a story
they tell me to take them at their word
i solemnly swear to tell their truth

america   as much a problem in metaphysics as
immortality   the nation of lost heads   rolled into
the galaxy like stars   each one a grain of sand in
the night's deep pockets   good morning   they say when
they wake   many faces go bad   go missing in the dark

today   crowds gather   in the streets   people
light fireworks   eat hot dogs   eyes red   they paint
their faces blue   don their gunpowdered wigs
for the parade   they sing the land of the free until it
hurts   their art   is pain suffered and outlived

what to a slave is the fourth of july   when
resurrection falls on the third   steadfast faith
americans believe in life   but only   in life after
death   they say   the only free man is a dead man
and in this way gain life everlasting

i am attracted to the promise of this land
its hunger   dances naked on the table   i touch
the mouth of its decadent poverty   i sit on the face
of its music   it leaves the taste of metal on my lips
sky falls   clouds melt   i write this page of snow

confess i present these findings to you   without
an objective lens   i solely report that for which we
have language   the rest   i cannot penetrate or name
in the end   *i speak against silence*
though it is silence   that moves me   to speak

Door of the Cosmos

I am not in life or love but a voyeur.
When there was something to believe in
I believed, and now that there is nothing,
I believe in nothing. I had been taught
how to be perfect but not how to live.
I ride in a rainbow-sherbet spaceship.
On replay, the cockpit blasts
A Tribe Called Quest's "The Space Program."
The Milky Way is an ocean of black coffee
holes. From the observation deck, I observe
how the men carry woe atop their heads.

II

Did you know that life has given love a guarantee

To last through forever and another day

Just as time knew to move on since the beginning

And the seasons know exactly when to change

STEVIE WONDER, "As"

Springtime Again

after Sun Ra as well as Danez Smith's "summer, somewhere"

Again, a spring in the step of boys
headed to meet their maker.

A swagger, a darkness sprung
with the obsession of flies.

Sunflower seeds litter god's front porch,
the yard overrun with dandelions,

yellow starbursts picked over for the pinks.
Again, snow. Angels. Girls named Hope and Faith,

their braids capped with black and gold beads,
glimmer of fireflies affixed with rubber bands.

The stork is actually a blue-footed
booby. The babies. Come alive.

Summer and Sally Walker
swaddled in brown liquor.

Johnnie takes his spirits neat,
ice uncalled for at winter's end.

*

Why must I chase the C.R.E.A.M.?
'Cause cat rules everything around me,

young blood in young world of
pussy-whipped buffoons. I see you;

can you see me watchin' you lovin' it?
Whether by microscope or telescope,

my body of work is accustomed to gaze.
An in-between state contributes greatly

to a country of longing. When in flux,
I have a strong constitution.

I no longer have a home in the present,
my sleeping bag splayed on Dante's fire

escape. The circles of hell are a Spenserian
stanza, a rhyme scheme of *Uhh! Na nah na nah.*

When judgment comes, ain't nowhere to run.
April snow is how time disciplines its children.

                                                        *

Pride cometh before. The fall.
The redheaded oaks made our

blood boil. I don't believe god
was ready to call me home, but

now was as good a time as any.
When asked my regrets,

I just remembered, remembered
freedom was life's great lie,

remembered *body* is another
word for *cage,* remembered

night knew my name before
I ever had reason to fear.

Some days are measured by caesuras,
some hours by snakes in the grass.

Only a foolish king would
mistake the forest for the trees.

                              *

This is how we are reborn:
come resurrection Sunday,

we pour out. A trail of Cadillacs,
rabbit feet and gator teeth hung

from rearview mirrors. The trunks
thumping so loud it's enough

to wake the dead, to dust the dirt
from shoulders, to make room

for the elbows and capsized knees.
In the end we knew what was ahead.

Postapocalypse was our present tense.
We sold key chains at the pearly gates,

light-up toys, and airbrushed T-shirts
one for ten or three for twenty. The hustle

never dies, it just changes, and the more
things change the more they stay the same.

Metamorphoses

Just as seasons change,
I shimmy-shimmy-yay,
a four-way call put on hold.

I hope to someday be free
from the tyranny of small
minds. I dart and dodge.

I keep evolving, shape-
shifting from woman to
man and back again, taking

oversexed snakes as my guide.
I am transformed each day
that I draw nearer to death.

The Tiresias myth is tired,
as is the lore that I sewed
my baby into my thigh.

Second comings are more
intense than the first.
A milkman hangs from my

right breast, my back a choke-
cherry tree. An ant has no
quarrel with a boot, a violin

doesn't play a bow. I saw my
reflection as a mare in beast
mode, a result of natural causes.

Hymn of Inscape

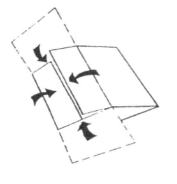

V. AN IDIOT BOX

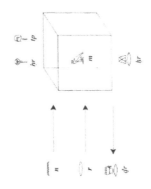

VI. A DEAD LANGUAGE

Liberation is both
a closing and an opening.
The concave Black body,
an argument turned inward.

My mother is claustrophobic
in tight spaces. As a child,
my father threw his brother down
the basement stairs in a box.

*The television is sometimes called
an "idiot box" from the Greek
for "private person," from
idios, meaning "one's own."*

Chinese boxes are made
in such a way as to show
the relationship of inclusion.
I am fluent in English only.

They're on to us.
There is an upside to being
a bottom. Unfettered,
we bond through bondage.

Is a dead language worth
studying? I am learning
hieroglyphics at Brown
(at the age of thirty-four).

I learned of Gerard Manley
Hopkins's coining of *instress*
and *inscape* via the Chinese
Scottish writer Jay G. Ying.

To be only one's own in an
enclosure is idiotic. A hymn
is a song or ode in praise or
honor of god, a nation, etc.

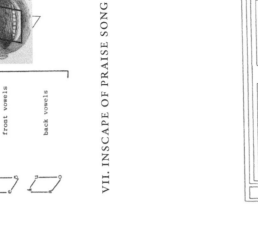

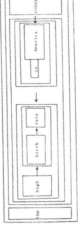

VII. INSCAPE OF PRAISE SONG

VIII. A CHINESE BOX

The inclusion of one element
in another forms a constituent.
The inclusion by one element of
another forms a construction.

Heidegger raises his hand to state,
"And in our being with one another
we would be time—
everyone and no one."

I hope to not be lost to history.
I pray to be a little-known Black
history fact. There is no fear in
resurrection.

A boy is a voice box, a larynx.
[A safe house] A man is a window-
less wall the human frame hangs on.
America is far from beautiful.

Clang! Derrida inquires,
"What is it to *have time?*"
In the meantime, I debate
if I'm possessed or a possession.

Have you seen or heard of
Lear Green? She escaped
in an old sailor's chest to
marry the man she loved.

In *Time Is a Mother,*
Ocean Vuong writes,
*Not an answer but an entrance
the shape of an animal. Like me.*

The Trap Music Museum
is filled with ministers of
music. A pretty pink
Cadillac, the getaway car.

Black Bell

A bell's dome represents the whole universe, the flat bottom represents the earth, and the hollow inside represents the space between the rest of the universe and the earth. When you strike a bell it sends a message from Earth out into the universe. Before reading, strike a bell tuned to G, the note connected to the throat chakra.

Your hand on my
music maker. My nipple
rings, comes to life in your mouth.

Hold fast onto my body. Unfasten
longing from my nape, as though
noise can only be joyful.

*

Black bell spoke out of turn.
In turn, the bells trilled with fiery fury,
a virtuous, vaginal vibrato.

When black bell starts to sound off,
it's a turn-on. Her sounds of a promising
silence. Not hopeful, but hopeless.

Over the Rainbow

Through the rain, I watch a woman
undress to "Blue in Green."

She places my name on the back of a chair.
Limp. Three syllables slump over, fall short.

The command center, her face,
a handbook of human motivations.

Cars honk from the secondhand streets
as the horn wipes away my fingerprints.

I reach out. She touches herself. Feels me.
Growing distant as though going the distance.

Two cicadas dangle from my gay lobes like head-
phones, hang down like the lightbulb's breast.

Under the bed, government bugs ear-hustle.
Indigo walls make the room [a stanza] a skybox.

This poem, a paper airplane. From the cobalt,
I listen for E-40 to tell me when to go.

A patient patient. She tries to unhear
my name inside her. Not soon enough,

I will leave, but first I want to see
how touch sounds out the wind's pain.

Bridge between Starshine and Clay

for Lucille Clifton

The bridge of the song
is meant to feel different.
To illustrate how I got over,

use a new key, a new chord
progression or time signature.
The bridge is not the end

but a cue to the chorus
to circle back around.
Here come the tragic

Greeks masked in African
finery, an offbeat dance
of appropriation. Good

artists copy, great artists
steal. My legs and hands
cupped, I throw at

the potter's wheel.
Ode to a Grecian urn,
from the dust and salt

of the earth, you were
formed. At first, your
body—blank verse.

Verse comes from
the Latin *vertere,*
which means "to turn."

To turn over a new leaf,
a new page,
with or without you,

the show must go on.
The never-ending story
has already begun.

Time with Stevie Wonder in It

after Christopher Gilbert

Picture Teddy Pendergrass
in fox-fur coat with hood.
So fresh, the trees are so clean of
their foliage. A thick beard
forms canopy for full lips.
The music man smolders.
The cold finds him untouchable.
He stands in front of a docked boat,
the sharp crease of his camel slacks
cut an angle. One leg crossed over
the other. The toe of a brown gator
boot, pointed as punctuation.
The white water, powdered sugar.
Two arms appear through slits of red fur.
Right hand clasped atop the left,
pinky ring and bracelet iced out.
Winter shakes its rigid tongue
at the singer's closed mouth.
The face of a gold watch peeks
from a sweater sleeve's synapse.
If this were just a poem,
there would be a certain timelessness—
the punch-clock Midwest would go on
clicking, the interval between ticks
like a ponderous void of living,
but what we have is much more than
they can see, much more than
a photograph can capture,
a still image that remains on
repeat, song still playing, long after
the vinyl clock has melted.

The Clearing

for JJJJJerome Ellis

Watch the gap. Rupture.
A verb, with wings split open,
stutters, splinters speech.
In the clearing is an absence.
An absent home is a house
abandoned before its time.
In our home, house music plays.
MUSICK is a clock of Snow.
The snowman catches the beat.
The beat drops a woman off
at the back door of her house.
The snare drum waits in the car.
Our extemporaneous ears exert.
Our eyes, an enclosed exposure.
You are hiding in the clearing
as punch line, an open concept
the mind apprehends
as though it were second nature.
To set the subject free we give it
a new cut, a new color, a new hairdo!
The tresses stress as they
quicken to capture the light.
You dare to silence, to slow down
the rhythm that blues my body.
Quickening. You might think it is
a question of speed, to be in time
not on time, how we all are
at the mercy of sound.

Climate Crisis Could Kill Off Great Tits, Scientists Warn

The birds got over on us,
which made our stomachs

turn, so bent on becoming
snakes. To make ends meet,

god said, *Come as you are,*
which meant tit for tat.

Once in a wild, the water
learns from our mistakes.

Lopsided harbinger of sag,
it was not the pitter-patter

heart, but the skitter-scatter
rhythm of survival. The tits

teeter, seesaw back and forth
on the brink of extinction.

Honeysuckle knows hunger
is more commonplace when

housed in a garden of change.
You, tater-tot hummingbird,

could be gone in the blink of
a mouth. Bite-size is how

god sees you, though small
minds make great expectations.

To warn is to predict the future,
to rid the foreskin of foresight.

A Song by Any Other Name

1–20 song-birds (singing-birds, songsters), | Listen:

1–3 | you hate to see it.

crows): | Let me rope you in.

1 | Among the **(2)** blacks

2 | is misery enough, God knows,

3 | but no poetry.

4 the starling (pastor, shepherd bird)

5 | No **(14)** nestled in a nest of sonnets.

6–8 | In the sticks, the crown

6 and 7 | lost its head. In a cloud

6 | of sweet rain was a lyric, tuned in to the keyhole

7 | stars. I've yet to speak of

8 | voice as instrument.

9 | To do so, I would have to sound off.

10 | Unladylike. On account of my seedy character,

11 | the early **(5)** gets the worm.

12 | About fifty-**(11)** times

13–17 | I have been dragged.

13 the blackbird | tip trills.

14 the nightingale (*poet.* |) is epic in scope.

15 | God said, **(3)** is what I'm afraid of.

16 the song thrush (*poet.* |) set free in verse.

17 | Lily-white,

18 and 19 | the mountain and the sky

18 | lark | are at each other's throat.

19 | Beyond what I can imagine,

20 | night is backwash—
a swallow

52

A Gentle Dialogue between Eternity and the Hours

I hate the phrase *relatively soon.*
Almost a year ago today, I lost my head,
but then again, time is relative.

My mind, that certain *je ne sais quoi,*
was never to be found again.

A relative once told me,
Don't never write nothing down,
file it all up top!

Make the devil kill two birds with one stone—
finch is one *l* away
from *flinch,*

what we do at
death's soft hands.

Topography of Silence

Do you picture heaven
dead quiet? The volume,
not the quantity of persons

but the decibels of sound,
pitchfork tombstones tuned
to frequencies of kinfolk.

I once made a mental map
(true to scale) of the afterlife.
Mountains high, valleys low,

waterways bifurcated by
bond rather than blood.
Silence, a parting gift.

The word *bed* is in the shape of itself.
A poem is a flower bed of needles.
Needless to say. Say less.

Garden of the Gods

As a matter of black,
I will trade a mountain
for a river. What does

that tell you about my
makeup? I once met a
cowboy. I said, *Let me*

hold your body. You know
I'm good for it. He gave his
consent. I wore him out.

On paper-thin sheets
I scissored a woman,
her expression hard

as a rock. She—a cliff
dweller, a figurehead
alien to my bizarre

beauty. I—a queer mare,
a stallion in the hands
of an angry god.

To be human is to be
homeless, the furthest
removed from grandeur.

I've met my makers in
flower beds of milkweed.
No birds-of-paradise

were there, only crows
dark as echoes, juniper
trees alive with want,

coyotes aroused by the
sound of cold glass. Between
me and the world is a wind

section of awe; inside me,
a desert of thistle. I've had
enough of the belief in

numberless fish, in
something other than
longhorn skulls.

Next to the vermilion
spires I feel small, my
nature second to none.

Watch the gods scurry like
daddy longlegs, moved
by a higher power.

SONG COMPOSED BY
HENRY BOX BROWN,
— ON HIS —
ESCAPE FROM SLAVERY.

AIR—UNCLE NED.

I.

Here you see a man by the name of Henry Brown,
Ran away from the South to the North,
Which he would not have done but they stole all his rights,
But they 'll never do the like again.
  Chorus—Brown laid down the shovel and the hoe,
      Down in the box he did go,
      No more Slave work for Henry Box Brown,
      In the box by *Express* he did go.

II.

Then the orders they were given and the cars they did start,
Roll along—Roll along—Roll along,
Down to the landing where the steamboat met,
To bear the baggage off to the North.
  Chorus—Brown laid down the shovel and the hoe,
      Down in the box he did go,
      No more Slave work for Henry Box Brown,
      In the box by Express he did go.

III.

When they packed the baggage on they turned him on his head,
There poor Brown liked to have died,
There were passengers on board who wished to set down,
And they turned the box down on its side.
  Chorus—Brown laid down the shovel and the hoe,
      Down in the box he did go,
      No more Slave work for Henry Box Brown,
      In the box by Express he did go.

IV.

When they got to the cars they throwed the box off,
And down upon his head he did fall,
Then he heard his neck crack, and he thought it was broke,"
But they never throwed him off any more.
  Chorus—Brown laid down the shovel and the hoe,
      Down in the box he did go,
      No more Slave work for Henry Box Brown,
      In the box by Express he did go.

V.

When he got to Philadelphia they said he was in port.
And Brown he began to feel glad,
And he was taken on the wagon and carried to the place,
And left "this side up with care."
  Chorus—Brown laid down the shovel and the hoe,
      Down in the box he did go,
      No more Slave work for Henry Box Brown,
      In the box by Express he did go.

VI.

The friends gathered round and asked if all was right,
As down on the box they did rap,
Brown answered them saying "yes, all is right,"
He was then set free from his pain.
  Chorus—Brown laid down the shovel and the hoe,
      Down in the box he did go,
      No more Slave work for Henry Box Brown,
      In the box by the Express he did go.

3 feet and 1 inch long, 2 feet wide, 2 feet and 6 inches high.

HYMN OF THANKSGIVING
SUNG BY
HENRY BOX BROWN,

After being released from his confinement in the Box at Philadelphia.

I waited patiently, I waited patiently for the Lord, for the Lord,
  And he inclined unto me, and heard my calling :
I waited patiently, I waited patiently for the Lord,
  And he inclined unto me, and heard my calling :
And he hath put a new song in my mouth,
Ev'n a thanksgiving, Ev'n a thanksgiving, Ev'n a thanksgiving unto our
  God.
Blessed, Blessed, Blessed, Blessed is the man, Blessed is the man,
  Blessed is the man that hath set his hope,   his hope in the Lord ; |
O Lord my God, Great, Great, Great,
Great are the wondrous works which thou hast done,
Great are the wondrous works which thou hast done, which thou hast
  done,
Great are the wondrous works.
Great are the wondrous works,
Great are the wondrous works, which thou hast done.
If I should declare them and speak of them, they should be more, more
            more than I am able to express.
I have not kept back thy loving kindness and truth from the great con-
  gregation.
I have not kept back thy loving kindness and truth from the great con-
  gregation.
Withdraw not thou thy mercy from me,
Withdraw not thou thy mercy from me, O Lord;
Let thy loving kindness and thy truth always preserve me.
Let all those that seek thee joyful and glad,
Let all those that seek thee, be joyful and glad, be joyful, be glad, be joy-
      ful and glad, be joyful, be joyful, be joyful, be joyful, be joy-
      ful and glad, be glad in thee.
And let such as love thy salvation,
And let such as love thy salvation, say always,
The Lord be praised.
The Lord be praised :
Let all those that seek thee be joyful and glad,
And let such as love thy salvation, say always,
The Lord be praised,
The Lord be praised,
The Lord be praised.

Elegy for Dred Scott

Dred dons penny loafers,
a bronze coin slid
in the slit of each eyelid.
Legs. Cross-examinations.

Theretofore, the verdict
stands on feet that wear
knockoffs, laced with twine
from the butcher.

Ergo error. There go
the facts, floating
facedown, a result
of riotous rulings.

Heretofore, a house is a
courtyard of citizenship,
a slave ship—
burden of proof.

For the sake of argument,
dread is embodied,
a private, public persona.

Whereas Dred asks us
to read the room,
a logistical night-
mare of legalities.

To air out the force of
brutality's bowels,
we lock eyes with
dread across the aisle.

In a poem, a straw man
is a no-brainer.
One courts the law
with flowered fists.

Dred draws up his
knees with black pen.
Dread, a knot penciled
in his stomach.

St. Louis Blues

Old-school players to new-school fools
posted up along the Mississippi River.

The city unites us in our derision.
We swim the Delmar Divide and decide

which world to enter, the palms
of our hands fractured street maps.

The houses' faces are missing brick-teeth,
cavities of have-nots at the roots.

For play-play, god made the Gateway Arch a swing.
Handy pushes gently, so I don't spill my pop,
pineapple Vess gives piss a run for its money.

The *C* of my middle name stands for Canada.
On the outskirts of Forest Park,
I was born a maple leaf rag.

A work of fire, a little star, shot out one day before
the Fourth of July. By far, I'd rather be a comet, but

I'm a wife now, with fingers full of diamond rings,
a husband with a heart hard as a rock cast in the sea.

All day, men drink, and women cry
over lost love and love lost.

You don't get to hate St. Louis.
You don't get to hate it unless you love it.

III

But that's getting too far ahead of the story, almost to the end,

although the end is in the beginning and lies far ahead.

RALPH ELLISON, *Invisible Man*

A Bell Is a Bearer of Time

**To be performed with bells on. All "writing" is performance,
some performance is "writing."*

I am
a product
of my time.
Time is a body
that resembles
a sound without a scale.
Forever, foreclosed fortitude.
In heaven, the dinner bell rings
as elegy. The porch-light stars turn
on their mothering moths. Betrayal
takes at least two, and wherever two
or more are gathered, I am there in
their pulsating timbre. To hear is to hunger
for the gendered race of sound. In my midst,
loneliness listens. In confidence, I am secreted
away. I was today years old when I learned the truth:
a dumbstruck bell is an idiophone. The strike made
by an internal clapper or an external hammer, a uvula—
that small flesh, conical body projecting downward from
the soft palate's middle. Vocal, vibrating vulva. I am less a writer
who reads than a reader who writes. Therein lies the trouble, the treble clef of
conviction. Come now to the feast of hearing, where Hortense J. Spillers gives a
sermon: *We address here the requirements of literacy as the ear takes on the functions of "reading."*
Call me bad news bear of bestial becoming. Some find me titillating, bare on the stage.
In "Venus in Two Acts," Saidiya Hartman asks, *Must the future of abolition be
first performed on the page?* Must I write a run-on of runaways?
Must you make out my handwriting? Evidence that loss has limbs.
The clawed syntax. The muzzled grammar. Don't be afraid.
Kill me with your language. Learn how to mark my
words.*

Idiophone, or Memory Is a Strange Bell

Fist to [face | fist | cuffs],
the [strobe | spot | flash] light
dances across the floor.

To [see | read | hear]
is to look [for | at | through] god.
We [wait | pray | cry]

to attend to our tuning.
At the [edge | end | close], you
deny me [pleasure | release | closure].

If a bell is a bottled poem
with frequencies of funk,
do you [smell | feel | hear] me?

To [remix | appropriate | steal]
is another way to pay homage to
your [mother | native | silver] tongue.

The photograph of the [house | church | school]
wreathed in kudzu vines of nostalgia
reminds me—memory mows a mile a minute.

My image is [immersive | still | moving].
Stand in the [nude | nuance | nut grass]
and see if you're not on [one | top | fire].

In the key to a life of [sin | sex | song],
the devil, disguised as a do-gooder,
[conducts | directs | misleads] the choir.

If they come [for | at | between] us,
we [glitch | glitch | glitch] until
we blow the speaker out of

the [sound | solar | nervous] system.
Sounds migrate [from | by | via]
[air | land | sea].

The [light | sound | ocean] waves
all wait for your call.
Telephone. It's Ol' Dirty.

He wants to give [you | me | us] *directions
home. Said it won't be too long.
Fly away to heaven, brother.*

Save a [place | space | seat] *for me.*
Calls are free after [nine | death | all].
[Please | Pleas]. *Put in a word for me.*

Letter from the End of the World

after Lisel Mueller

The reason no longer matters,
the why, the how—irrelevant,
the politicians, the smooth
of my love's bald head, him
saying *It's okay to be sad*.

The point is I miss crab legs,
fried chicken, and french fries.

I sat in my house for days,
all I wanted was to go home.

At first the mountains seemed
to bid me good riddance,
the trees tired of everything
I represent.

But I learned to study the stars,
to tuck my chin when I jump
from high places.

I learned the sun does not owe
me a single thing, that I am what
I take for granted.

Race—a product of a sick imagination,
the point is I wasn't right
to begin with.

I started out as a girl
without a shadow of
a doubt, my opposable
thumbs at the ready.

At the end of the world
I was bananas, a woman
with a mouth full of golds.

If you don't like this ending,
implore the children to
make up one of their own.

Live Long and Prosper

My mother taught me to sit back,
wait for people to tell on themselves.
In silence, I raise the lightsaber.
At my mouth, a blue freezer pop
in plastic sleeve. A sugar-drip IV.
If you wish to be alive on arrival,
do not come unless I send for you.

A Child Is like a Clarinet

for Eliza Harris and Henri Akoka

Similes are dangerous.
To equate a person to

an object, an instrument
no less, is a risk.

A child is like a clarinet.
A mother is like a clarinetist.

Personhood posits
promising possibilities.

Poems are willing to die.
Poems dare, just as Eliza

Harris leaped onto pieces
of ice to cross the frozen

Ohio River with her baby
in her hands. Poems flee,

just as Henri Akoka
jumped onto the top of

a moving train with his
clarinet under his arm.

One of these things
is not like the other.

Can't you tell? Mouthpiece
from lips, flesh from wood.

Author's Womb as Bell

YOKE

CROWN

HEAD

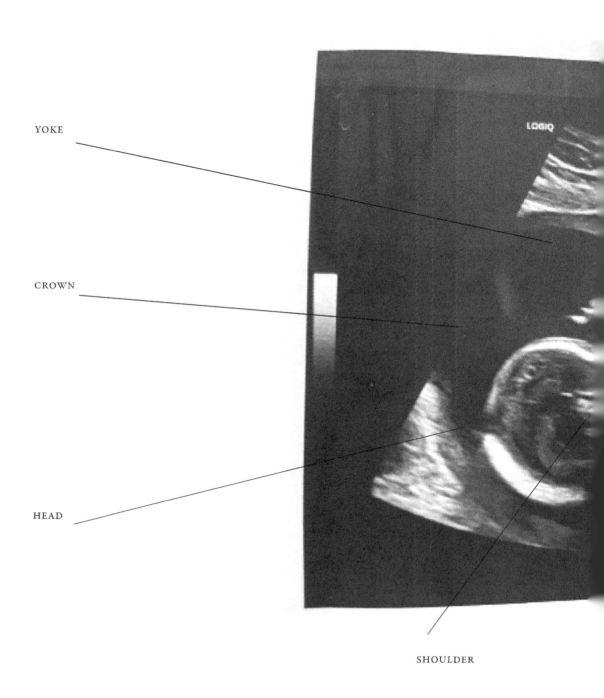

SHOULDER

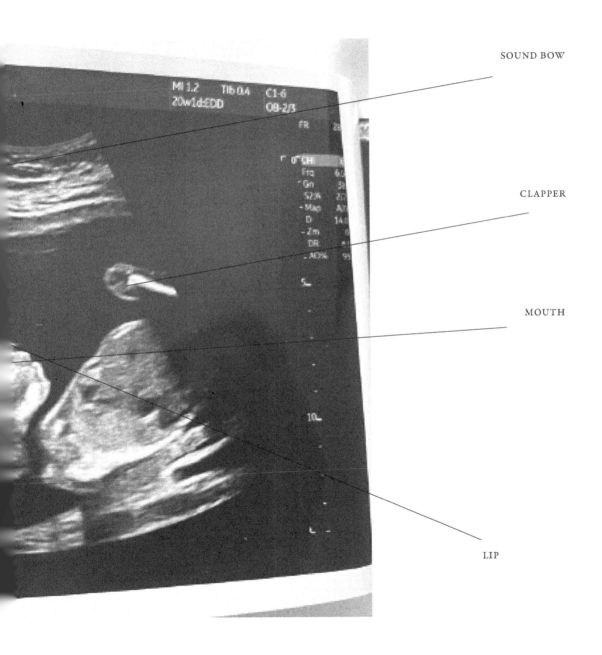

SOUND BOW

CLAPPER

MOUTH

LIP

The Budding Soul

for Cécile Sauvage

A pregnant poet composes
with the help of nipples'

notation. Music milks as
the needle latches down.

A father is a translator,
the son a translation.

A composer is born
via surrogate songbird.

Lyric imprinted
as the earth turns

on the wobbly grooves
of a tired mother's face.

A life-form forms a life
not unlike a flower.

Is the ovary human?
The stigma conscious?

The soul in bud,
disembodied?

Black Bell

A bell's dome represents the whole universe, the flat bottom
represents the earth, and the hollow inside represents the
space between the rest of the universe and the earth. When
you strike a bell it sends a message from Earth out into the
universe. Before reading, strike a bell tuned to E, the note
connected to the solar-plexus chakra.

If you look the sound
dead in its mouth,

you will see that it smells
like the eyes of spoiled eggs—

like a moment, passed too quickly
and not quickly enough.

You will find black bell
in a mess of trees, where

time barks and leaves
offerings of yellow gold,

where the blackbirds
blanket the blackened river,

where one can barter
with their peace in pieces.

Another way of saying
you are not your flesh,

further proof that
loneliness has hands.

Black bell is the space inside her.
Hollowed. Hallowed. Halo.

John Cage Meets Sun Ra

featuring Rita Dove

Deadpan. A silent solo
of empty words. Blue

in green gestures, we
hold this myth to be

potential. What was
never an issue before

is previously unissued,
which brings us to

the question of voice.
Nothing more, nothing

less. Self-evident.
The damned air.

Lord of lyric, make me
your instrument.

If I can't be free,
make me a mystery.

Performance Directions

PREPARATORY INSTRUCTIONS

To perform the next poem, "For Henry 'Box' Brown, from Alison 'Inbox' @ Brown," You (the Reader) will need the sixty envelopes created to read the poem "Hymn of Inscape." You will also need a mirror, a medium-sized metal box that is see-through and labeled "EXPRESS MAIL," and a large table or surface. Arrange the envelopes on the table or surface so that each feeling can be easily read. To the right of the envelopes place the mirror and the metal box.

AUDIENCE INSTRUCTIONS

These steps are to be executed in collaboration with the audience at the moment in the poem marked "Intermission/Intervention." At this time, invite the audience to come to the table and look at all your feelings on display. Instruct the audience members to each choose one enveloped feeling. Inform the audience that they should not open the envelope; this can be emphasized by warning them that it is a federal crime to open mail that is intended for someone else. One at a time, each audience member should then say the feeling they have chosen aloud while looking very closely into the mirror. The audience member will then place the envelope inside the box to post their "express mail." Once these steps are complete, the audience members can return to their seats.

YOUR INSTRUCTIONS

When everyone is reseated, You will read the remainder of the poem. Once You have completed the poem, You will collect the envelopes from the metal box, then say the following, "A performative reading (this time with feeling) starts now . . ." Next, You will read off each of the feelings. As You read each feeling, remove the piece of paper from inside the envelope. After You have read all the feelings, read each of the pieces of paper as an improvised version of the poem "Hymn of Inscape," this time collectively crafted with the audience.

For Henry "Box" Brown, from Alison "Inbox" @ Brown

In seeing there is love, in being seen there is abhorrence.

KOBO ABE, *The Box Man*

In the spring of 1849,
Henry "Box" Brown (enslaved)
shipped himself from Richmond to Philadelphia
in a crate lined with a coarse woolen cloth.

[172 years later]
In the summer of 2021, Alison "Inbox" @ Brown was activated
via email. She then moved, by car, from Colorado Springs
to Providence by way of Chicago by way of St. Louis.

In the fall of 2021, the artist RaMell Ross
freight shipped himself from north to south:
Rhode Island to Hale County, Alabama.

Henry "Box" Brown's box had the following dimensions:
3 feet long by 2 feet 6 inches deep by 2 feet wide.

RaMell Ross was in a 4 by 4 by 8 feet box
on an open air, gooseneck trailer.
The contracted driver was not aware of the crate's contents.

Alison "Inbox" @ Brown rode with her fiancé and belongings
in a tightly packed Chevrolet Spark for approximately 29 hours.

Henry "Box" Brown traveled for 27 hours
labeled as dry goods, via Adams Express Company.
There was a hole cut in the box for air.

RaMell Ross's 59-hour trip was video recorded in full. Inside, Ross began
the *Black Dictionary* (aka *RaMell's Dictionary*), which involved Ross writing
the word "black" before every entry in a childhood dictionary.

In the spring of 2022, at the Steel Yard in Providence,
Alison "Inbox" @ Brown built a metal box, the size of her head,
in homage to Henry "Box" Brown.

The day Brown was to escape—to get out of work—
he burned his hand to the bone with sulfuric acid.

After a semester of graduate poetry workshops,
one Sunday at the Steel Yard, Alison "Inbox" @ Brown
burned her finger with an arc while welding.

In large words, *THIS SIDE UP* was written on
the outside of Henry "Box" Brown's box.
On several occasions, the box was turned
upside down and handled roughly.

Alison "Inbox" @ Brown spent many hours
fashioning a metal box that the audience
could see through.

Thinking about Henry "Box" Brown
had Alison "Inbox" @ Brown
in her feelings.*

*According to urbandictionary.com,
the phrase *in my feelings* means
"emotional, thinking about stuff."

Are you beginning to catch feelings*
for Alison "Inbox" @ Brown?

*According to urbandictionary.com,
the phrase *catch feelings* means
"to begin to like someone (romantically),
usually unexpectedly."

To catch and return a runaway
elicited feelings of gratitude
and great reward, by-products of
the 1850 Fugitive Slave Act.

In 1773, *Poems on Various Subjects, Religious and Moral*
by Phillis Wheatley, Negro Servant to Mr. John Wheatley,
of Boston, in New England was published.

[250 years later]
In 2023, Alison "Inbox" @ Brown
earned a graduate degree in poetry from Brown University
and signed a contract to publish her second poetry collection.

Thomas Jefferson argued in response to Wheatley,
The compositions published under her name
are below the dignity of criticism.

Alison "Inbox" @ Brown hopes her work
warrants the dignity of criticism; however, she prays
that as a Black author she is not placed in a box.

Intermission/Intervention

Henry "Box" Brown's
box was made of wood.

Alison "Inbox" @ Brown's
box is made of steel.

Steal away
sounds like
steel away.

Autocorrect.
Henry "Box" Brown
was a real box man.

Alison "Inbox" @ Brown
is an artificial box man,
also known as a woman.

In a carefully calculated system,
Alison "Inbox" @ Brown is a statistic.
A calculator is a calculating box.
What are the costs to ship?

Alison "Inbox" @ Brown was once pregnant.
Her womb became a box, yet
she refused to become a statistic.
A statistic is a box, a rectangular calculation.

In 1850, Lear Green escaped to freedom
by shipping herself in an old sailor's chest
from Baltimore to Philadelphia
to marry the man she loved and
to ensure her children would be free.

In the summer of 2022, Alison "Inbox" @ Brown
flew, in an airplane, from Rhode Island to Colorado
to marry her betrothed in a town called Monument.

Years ago, Alison "Inbox" @ Brown fled her then-husband,
traveling from Virginia to Missouri, after dropping out of
a PhD program in English at Temple University in Philadelphia.

When Henry "Box" Brown arrived
in Philadelphia, and his box was opened,
he recited a psalm.

I waited patiently for the Lord,
and He heard my prayer.
Brown then began to sing.

Alison "Inbox" @ Brown stands before the Lord
as a survivor rather than a victim of domestic abuse.
A survivor is free. A victim is placed in a box.

It is unclear whether Henry "Box" Brown's
singing was the start, end, or continuation of
a performance.

Alison "Inbox" @ Brown is
obsessed with bringing Kobo Abe's novel
The Box Man to life, an IRL translation.

When Alison "Inbox" @ Brown arrived
in Providence, she was expected
to read her poems aloud.

In the spring of 2023, Alison "Inbox" @ Brown performed
this piece as the final for Professor Tracie Morris's course
Intertextuality, Interconnectivity: A Performative Sonnet Approach.

It is unclear whether Alison "Inbox" @ Brown's
reading is the start, end, or continuation of
a performance.

Henry "Box" Brown would go on to become
a magician, showman, and renowned performer,
often reciting the psalm he sang when he
first emerged from the box.

In the spring of 1850, Henry "Box" Brown's
Mirror of Slavery (a panorama)
opened in Boston and was exhibited
through the summer.

In the spring of 2022, Alison "Inbox" @ Brown debuted
"Mirror of Freedom" (a poem) in Providence.
It is playing until . . .

Queen Lear

The child emperor of Sunday,
full grown and dressed up
in invisible clothes. Eighteen
years, of ordinary size, she has
reason to be confident. Quick
speech, mouth pried open like
an oyster, love juices dribbling
salt and watered silk. Persuasion
is a scar on the side of a man's
face. Despite good-looking,
the missing remains like a
motherless child. Tragedy
is a matter of perspective.
Change your orientation,
shift one hundred
fifty degrees, and see
if you don't find a
REWARD.

$150 REWARD.—Ran away from the subscriber, on Sunday night, 24th instant, my NE-GRO GIRL, Loar Green, about 18 years of age, black complexion, round featured, good looking and of ordinary size; had on and with her when she left, a tan-colored silk bonnet, a dark plaid silk dress, a light mouselin de laine, also, one watered silk cape and one tan colored cape. I have reasons to be confident that she was persuaded off by a negro man named Wm. Adams, black, quick spoken, 5 feet 10 inches high, a large scar on one side of his face running down in a ridge by the corner of his mouth, about four inches long, barten by trade unt works mostly about taverns, opening oysters, &c. He has been missing about a week; he had been heard to say he was going to marry the above girl and ship to New York, where it is said his mother resides. The above reward will be paid if said girl is taken out of the State of Maryland and delivered to me; or fifty dollars if taken in the State of Maryland,   JAMES NOBLE,
m26 $1*5   No. 153 Broadway, Baltimore.

The Sun, Baltimore, Maryland, 28 May 1857

82

Got 'til It's Gone

To write is to place the reader on notice. To run is to leave an away message.

Close your projector-screen mouth. Lay down your soft palate in my arms.

An incision should speak slow. A quick flick of the wrist would set fire to the city.

Don't it always seem to go that you don't know what you've got 'til it's gone.

Disparu French for "faded away." Masculine past tense now in vogue at the balls.

Genteel, the sky was more a copper color, the waxing crescent moon a Roman nose.

Notice.

I will give TEN DOLLARS reward, for apprehending, delivering or confining in Jail so that I get him, my negro man DAVE, who ranaway on the 14th inst. he is of yellow complexion, slow spoken and about 5 feet 5 inches high, with a scar on his right arm, I believe occasioned by an incision made by a Doctor on each side the leading vein that runs down to he thumb, 5 inches above his wrist:— Dave is about 18 or 20 years of age and has a full, projecting mouth; I expect he will try to pass in white men's clothing.

DEMPSEY SPRUILL.

Edenton Gazette and North-Carolina General Advertiser, Edenton, North Carolina, 6 July 1829

ONE HUNDRED DOLLARS REWARD—For the delivery of BRAZILE, in either of the city prisons. He run away last July; has been seen dressed in women's clothes several times in the city, and also in genteel male apparel; he is a regular attendant of the balls, speaks French and English, is about 21 years old, a dark mulatto or copper color, has a Roman nose, rather slender, genteel person. He formerly belonged to Henry Hopkins, Esq., of this city. He came from Charleston, South Carolina, five years ago, and — the Charleston brogue when speaking English. Inquire at No. 73 Baronne street.

GEO. A. BOTTS.

The Daily Picayune, New Orleans, Louisiana, 1 January 1849

83

$15 REWARD.—Absconded from the subscriber, on the 15th instant, a mulatto woman RACHEL, aged about 40 or 45 years; had on an iron collar with three prongs, with a small bell attached to each prong. She wore away a red calico frock and red shawl. It is supposed she will attempt to go to Frankfort, Kentucky. The above reward will be paid to any person who will lodge her in any jail in the State, or deliver her to me, No 53, Bourbon street. Institution.
J F BUFFET
1817. 8t

The Daily Picayune, New Orleans,
Louisiana, 19 February 1844

COMMITTED to the Jail of *Chesterfield*, a middle sized black Fellow who says his Name is JOHN, and has a Flower in his Forehead made in the Form of a Diamond, with Specks down to the End of his Nofe; he had on an Ofnabrug Shirt, and a Pair of fhort Ofnabrug Breeches. He fays he came from the *Weft Indies*, and was fold; but cannot, or will not, tell his Mafter's Name. The Owner is defired to prove his Property, pay Charges, and fetch him away.
JAMES BALL, Jailer.

Virginia Gazette (Purdie and Dixon),
Williamsburg, Virginia, 12 November 1772

Have you seen Rachel recently?
Last I heard, round her neck was
a three-pronged diamond necklace!

Last I seen,
she wore a raspberry beret,
red frock, and matching shawl.

Sharp as a whistle, slick as a tack,
she's cold-blooded!
Lord, deliver her! Absconded.

John was committed.
Committed to the idea of
remaining uncommitted.

When a fellow reaches
middle size, he comes
into his own, blossoms,

if you will, like a flower
on a forehead, a bud made
in the form of Mother Nature.

The Daily Picayune, New Orleans, Louisiana, 11 October 1837

North-Carolina Journal, Halifax, North Carolina, 23 October 1792

September left bearing gifts
of lusty leaves. That fall,
the people could fly,

due, in part, to their parrot-
toed feet. If the body fell
ill they just took off, went

high as the cheekbones
of a joyful noise. Absence
is a presence we detect.

Memory is a little dog,
nearly white, that follows
and answers to no one.

What clothes the wind wears
is uncertain. Wispy garments,
tolerably sensible.

Betwixt a straw hat
and the age of reason
is surely a charge of heart.

Look back at It

A man of letters eyes me
from across the way.
He—*Homo erectus*—sings
darkness back from the hills

of my unholy posterior.
The intoxicating clap of all
twofold things—hands, cheeks,
lips clasped together.

Want takes hold of creatures
big and small. Top to bottom
I trace his pointed supplications
with what god has entrusted to me

alone: a mouth that sways and drags,
wrested forth by the same song
of longing. I beg to be freed,
laden with a memory of horses.

And I—already half-dead—
take this man beside himself with
anguish. A trembling housed
in his single-minded fingers.

He dares me to beg for mercy,
until pain turns into pleasure,
as if something can be loved
beyond the certainty of change.

It is true.
He loves me in every way possible,
my labyrinth of unending mirrors,
my singular unfolding of his hunger.

The waiting on him is hard. It wears
on me like a harness.

Even the night must put in work.
Need and desire partition the day,
as I suck sugar from a wishbone's head.

I mount and ride him into a horse.
No man can serve two masters.

Cognitive Mapping

Like cartographers, the Language poets
hold tight to their non-sequitur ships.

Everything of importance has a key,
a legend of symbols, which suggests

my grandma's hands were signifiers.
Her geospatial Jell-O, sugar-free.

I stream the whole of her caps-lock knees
into the Internet Explorer of my bones.

I shift the state of my being to delete.
Where there is grief, call it a highway,

imagination, a narwhal in the river.
Take the sum of my parts, congruent to

the space in your compass arms.
Hug the protractor's enlarged belly.

Measure the angle of a mother's
cognitive map with tweets hashtagged

Northwest, the copyright of a biracial
child, blown out of proportion on the

Rolodex's neck, spinning like a map
with no colonies, the land surveyors

having all become beekeepers.
There is a man named Jobs in the machine,

perhaps a second cousin to Job. Divine
comedy. Potatoes are the preexisting text

of a giant's dirty toes,
sullied with allegory.

As a child, I painted pictures with my feet,
once even mapped Africa with my left hand,

the folds in the brain ambidextrous.
Our aversion to wrinkles, a reflection of our egos'

intentions. YKK on the face of zippered body
bags. Mountain ranges capped with ice,

these words cryogenic preservation.
A forest grown from the ashes of Walt Disney.

To name is to freeze.
To translate is to melt.

The best way to decode the environment is
with one's nose, one's nostrils well-read in

debris. Detritus. Horses have always been
astronomers, and billy goats, social-media trolls.

Science has shown that dogs can
understand one another's barks
regardless of where they come from,

and yet the way humans hear differs,
depending on language and culture.

Woof woof, the sound of patriotism.
Bow wow, a vulgar logic for wagging tails.

The web pages are uploading at a bandwidth
that I and this frame cannot support.

Ghosts are sound waves below human hearing,
road trips leading to empty-handed homes,

the cancer cells now traveling with GPS.
I am undressing in a window of doubt.

I am addressing a subject that
I know nothing about, except for

the fact that it
does not exist.

We Gave the Clock a Face

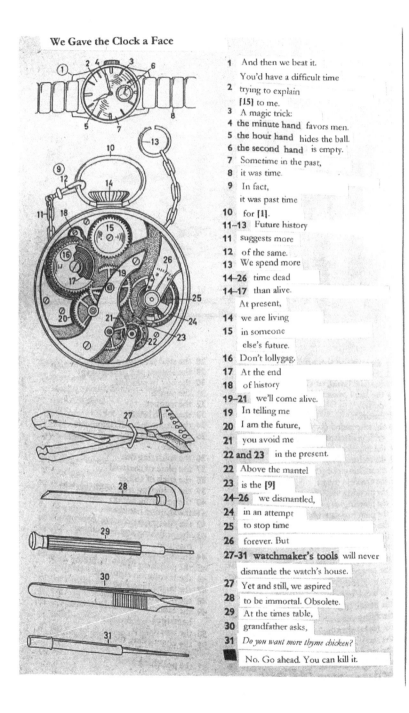

1 And then we beat it.

   You'd have a difficult time

2 trying to explain

   [15] to me.

3 A magic trick:

4 the minute hand favors men.

5 the hour hand hides the ball.

6 the second hand is empty.

7 Sometime in the past,

8 it was time.

9 In fact,

   it was past time

10 for [1].

11–13 Future history

11 suggests more

12 of the same.

13 We spend more

14–26 time dead

14–17 than alive.

   At present,

14 we are living

15 in someone

   else's future.

16 Don't lollygag.

17 At the end

18 of history

19–21 we'll come alive.

19 In telling me

20 I am the future,

21 you avoid me

22 and 23 in the present.

22 Above the mantel

23 is the [9]

24–26 we dismantled,

24 in an attempt

25 to stop time

26 forever. But

27–31 watchmaker's tools will never

   dismantle the watch's house.

27 Yet and still, we aspired

28 to be immortal. Obsolete.

29 At the times table,

30 grandfather asks,

31 *Do you want more thyme chicken?*

   No. Go ahead. You can kill it.

Keeping Time

Time had no chronological scaffold: no one was keeping time, nor did they seem to notice gravity.

GRETEL EHRLICH

My great-great-great-grandmamma could fly.
She kept time in architecture and anatomy
by tapping her palms at her sides,
flapping her feet like a herald heron.
She stuck her neck out so I could
breathe on land. Underwater:
you win some, you lose some.
Ancestors. Traveling up, there is
a vertical line that distinguishes
god from go(l)d. Parenthetical
wings are why the caged bird sings.
Behind its beak is a stone of a story,
spit out like asking for forgiveness
by force. The Gilded Age of America
is the period of permission, between
the gold-toothed smile of my kinfolk
and the shiver of sharks at their heels.

Hymn of Inscape

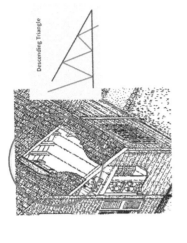

Descending Triangle

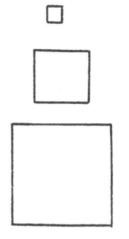

IX. *LOOPHOLE OR TRIANGLE OF RETREAT

X. ANGELS OF BREAD BOXES

A nation is an open secret.
Boys will be boys, never manly,
nevermore, never ever.
To escape is to sing.

Cut my hair in a box,
I mean a box fade,
to better frame my face
for when I meet my maker.

The fugitive wishes to be
left as they are found.
A woman:* a loophole.
A girl: a troubled treble clef.

Buried alive inside a sea-
shell of myself, shadowed
nostalgia, nationhood
the man cave I exited.

See Harriet Jacobs hiding
in plain sight [running
in place]. Secreted in a
crawl space of 9 feet by 7 feet,

See Henry "Box" Brown
in a box 3 feet by 2 feet long,
2 feet and 6 inches high,
labeled as dry goods.

3 feet at the highest point.
A garret is poetic justice.
A poem requests an audience of
none or a body of water.

Imagine the angels of bread boxes.
Brown had only one bladder of
water and a few biscuits.
Express yourself.

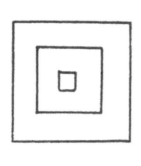

XI. AN OPEN SECRET

Don't turn water into whine, instead,
express-mail your tears with
the express purpose of
misrecognition. Optical illusion.

Androgynous mind's eye.
I'm going, going, back, back
to the end, to the womb of
a place where it all began.

If you look closely, each of
our navels is a keyhole.
Can you believe we made it
out alive? Expressly.

There is a science to the
magic trick of mind games,
to how my boxy brain got
tired of spinning in circles.

XII. KEYHOLE OF ESCAPE

A poem's lyrics are its palace
for the people, its lyric
a temple of thanksgiving.
I lift my vowels in praise.

How long can you
mishandle the situation
of a body, before
it up and disappears?

How much can you handle,
before you retreat from
mistreatment? Melodic
blood flows, lets loose

from the flesh, that
thick, clammy chord.
Logic is to illogic
as speech is to song.

95

IV

I pray God, that none like us ever may live again until time

shall be no more.

DAVID WALKER, *Walker's Appeal, in Four Articles, Together with a Preamble, to the Colored Citizens of the World, but in Particular and Very Expressly to Those of the United States of America* (1829)

Swing Low, Sweet Chariot

Because I could not stop for Death,
I creep. In a subjunctive mood,
I travel back to the future, to the
place where I hold out for a sound.

At present—I ride shotgun,
Eliot at the wheel of an Impala
with suicide doors. Immortality
kicks the back of my seat.

She rolls down her window
even though the air is on.
We pause at Sonia's house,
the one on the end with lions.

All the ghosts in her garden
have heart, the bees extinct,
and the Negroes high yellow in
pollen. 'Twas mercy brought

me from pagan poppies.
'Twas love that drove me
toward this climax of laden
light. I look away from

the pistil of war's flowered head.
There were birds where questions
should have been, in this world
with no use for gender.

T.S. rolls slow with a gangsta lean.
He points ahead, calls my hometown
the waste land. He kisses my head
and dust names me its daughter.

What the Lyric Be

Wordsworth, B-boy, beatbox vocal cord
code-switching through the wheat fields at daybreak
clicking teeth against the corn's high yellow thighs
prying open like the sunlight's tear ducts
on the morning the moon forgot how to speak Twi
the cicadas having screeched all night in Old English
like a man who has forgotten his name
calling out the leaves of grass as though
stalks of letters at right angles have meaning
a way of theorizing the rhetoric of beauty
a fig tree trembling at the rain's hungry lick
a finch weaving myth into a nested crown of logic
the wildflowers' arms on dial-up internet
a virgin using the petals as her service provider
he loves me, he loves me not, with every flick of her wrist
the wind knowing the typeface her lips are set in
pockmarked cheeks peppered with salt
the politics of resentment seasoning the spittle
true poems flee like a slave in Mississippi
googling "home" with no filter or cookies
the tuning fork having shorted in the eardrum's mouth
the devil was in the details when he read the star's hands
prongs of a serpent's embrace, steam dancing on
a cloud's rolled tongue, wet and pregnant
with words so soft the dirt could swallow the sound
what must we remember, to forget how we were born?
when we ask for advice, it is rather for permission
for we know not what we do when we do it in free will
a robot puts a conch shell to its lips and blows
a man puts a seashell to his ear and hears the ocean
tell a lie long enough and it will surely turn to truth

Ghost in the Machine

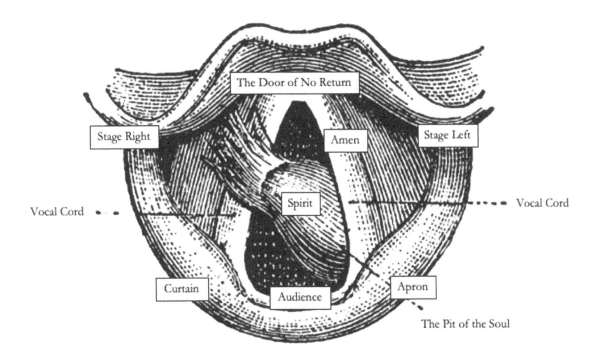

Labels in figure: The Door of No Return · Stage Right · Amen · Stage Left · Vocal Cord · Spirit · Vocal Cord · Curtain · Audience · Apron · The Pit of the Soul

A Recipe for the Common Task

for Nikolai Fyodorovich Fyodorov

To resurrect the dead through scientific means is the common task. Our religion is anti-death. We wish for the death of death. Love must fuse, not confuse. One should live with all and for all—meaning all people of all time. Universal physical resurrection of the dead due to advances in science and technology can be achieved via the following means.

PREP
87 years, 19 days, and 7 hours

BAKE
3 months

TOTAL
uncertain

YIELD
limitless

INGREDIENTS
4 car batteries
3½ cups unbleached all-purpose flour
1 monkey wrench
1 nursing bra
2 vessels
3 large eggs, at room temperature
1 copy of Henry Dumas's *Ark of Bones*
4½ cups dark brown sugar, tightly packed
8–10 fried chicken gizzards
1 tablespoon rum or the liqueur of your choice (optional)
1 copy of Joaquim Maria Machado de Assis's *The Posthumous Memoirs of Brás Cubas*
6 teaspoons fish sauce
82 toothpicks
16 soul or R & B albums in a milk crate
1½ cups prickly pear, diced into cubes
3 cups (equal parts) corn, squash, and beans
1 generous slice of 7UP pound cake
35 cotton balls

15 sticks of spearmint chewing gum
4 hotel pens
2 David Hammons snowballs
1 sewing needle

INSTRUCTIONS

1.

Preheat the oven to 124°F. Lightly grease a 16" × 7" oxidized sheet of copper and place it to the right. Arrange the complete skeleton of the deceased on the surface. If bones are not available, then ashes, a lock of hair, a piece of the deceased's clothing, a shoe, jewelry, eyeglasses, or toothbrush will suffice.

2.

Place a steel surgical table, on wheels, to the left. Set a living mammal, under anesthesia, on the disinfected surface. Insert a floppy disk between the limp lips of the animal. To dress the bestial up a bit, sift a shower of confectioners' sugar over its body. Add salt to taste.

3.

Use the charging cord for a cellular phone to connect the deceased and the animal. Be sure to first grease the application areas with Royal Crown hair dressing. Place the power plug directly into the stomach of the mammal. Using jumper cables, connect a chokecherry tree to the head of the animal and to the skull of the deceased thus forming triangulation between plant, animal, and human.

4.

To a large glass bowl, add a pinch of stinging nettle, meadow saffron, snowberry, herb of grace, red clover, shepherd's purse, woodland pinkroot, thorn apple, hedge hyssop, and some sweet potato peels. Place to the side. In a medium-sized wooden bowl, add four rusted nails, a wishbone, a prosthetic penis, a glass eye wearing a blue contact lens, a shot of squid ink, and a splash of ginger ale. Stir until a thick consistency.

5.

In a small metal bowl, beat three egg whites, jambool seeds, a hint of lemon juice, and two chicken feet until stiff peaks form. Sprinkle the fingernails of a murdered child (gone too soon) over the ashes of an elder (passed due to heart disease) and add to mixture. Refrigerate for two hours and thirty minutes. Next, stir in shredded coconut, three cowry shells, one teaspoon of drool from a bloodhound, and a black-and-white photograph of a stranger (soaked for at least twenty-four hours in bleach). Whisk to combine after each addition. Cover with velvet do-rag and let sit.

6.

Mix a few pieces of plastic gathered from the street, seven bottlecaps, eighty-seven drinking straws, three red-tailed hawk feathers, onion powder, garlic powder, chewing tobacco, Frederick Douglass's root, a deflated soccer ball, and a crawfish. Beat in the sugar gradually and add any remaining ingredients. After all ingredients are combined, apply to the surface area of the deceased. Use white lace gloves for a smooth application.

7.

To replace politics with physics requires knives. Cut a square from the right lung of a tuber-culosis patient, then slice a triangle from the left lung of an asthma sufferer. Place the square and triangle over the circular holes of the eye sockets. Insert the deceased, tree, and animal into the oven.

8.

After at least ninety days have passed, prepare for a spirit to enter, then ride, the deceased—life everlasting the crowning achievement.

The Body Faceup

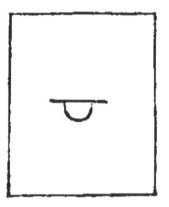

THE RESURRECTION OF HENRY BOX BROWN AT PHILADELPHIA.
Who escaped from Richmond Va. in a Box 3 feet long 2½ ft. deep and 2 ft wide.

Regeneration

after Suji Kwock Kim's "Generation"

0

Once, we were really something: once, we were twofold.

1

In the underworld, we heard history chugging along,
galloping like an unarmed horseman to war.

2

We heard human language,
motherless mouths opening and closing like the year's
doors, voices projecting sorry songs unheard of.
We heard words lip-synched in fear.

3

We felt unclean, sinful bodies sliding
down one another's chute-back,
wet, dark, lower, lower, facedown we floated again
across the River Styx. Not far from grief was solace.
If forgotten you die twice, then you are too far gone. Underwater.
Time is a debt to be paid in fluids. We took after it.
Bittersweet, the peaceful sleep we tasted, the eyelids gently closed,
             the headrest made of moss and pine needles:
bittersweet when remembered they exhume and exhume.

4

They called us over oceans of *landless acknowledgments,*
their voices gurgling with red dirt, our powdered blood,

a seasoned salt of triangular trade.
Fevers climbing, we hid in trees, and refused to come down.
We ran out of hope, we swam through possibilities. Exhausted.
One green day, we—the grateful dead—were roused.
They read our wrinkled fingertips like sour grapes.
It turns out when buried we grow live cultures.
Dragged, pulled by the underarms, hoisted like sacks of flour,
our muscles unraveled, stiff limbs twitched. We were truly something else.
We didn't want to be resurrected. We didn't want to come back alive.
Callously their hands groped for us through cemeteries of children,
coldly their hands tore us from ghosts' plump bosoms.
From mule bones and hard heads of corn,
quilted tissues, oxygen tanks, abandoned case files, metal drawers,
from boxes of hardened brown sugar, tins of grits, jars of used oil,
from cracks in concrete sidewalks,
                    the laugh of comeback kids pounding the pavement,
from dreams deferred and underway,
they dug us up.

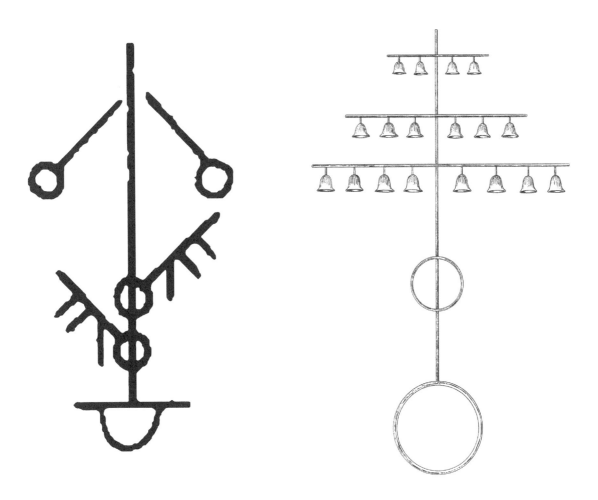

But for the Love of God

I am a woman. Undone,
a woman is a man.

I am a woman who gave birth
to the idea of a man who could
outdo himself only if he tried.

To make love to my namesake
I take up my strap like arms, for
in fact, she wants no part of any man.

To piggyback on the
mention of her pink:

I'm feelin' myself.
I'm feelin' myself.

There are women who have
cut off whole parts of them-

selves, and done it in
the name of love.

When I straddle a man
I too can get carried away.

In the holy book to come,
I have a cow as a horse;

you will die from laughter
at the sight. I have beat

a thing to death and called it
horseplay. As good as dead,

I'm not of this world but in it.
I began in no-man's-land, a nobody.

I waited for god to count me in,
to send me to a city made of fire.

Nine Circles of Hell (36 Chambers)

Limbo

Now you see me, now you don't.
A holy Ghostface Killah,
I arrived in the afterlife
by way of Bumblefuck, USA.

Don't shoot the haint.
At first it was unclear whether god
was friend or foe. No one had my back
at the rapture. No Harriet with sawed-off

shotgun was there to pull me
down from the white horse.
Did she pave the way for me
only to get caught up?

A floor model with no instructions,
I became my own manual. Beatrice or Bonita
Appelbaum, a virgin vigil, my better half
sent on my behalf, to guide me home.

Lust

Her legs up, a Vulcan salute.
An exercise in dexterity.
When god calls me a pussy,
I am what I eat.

How many times have I
been told that I am going
straight to hell? I lost count
after time turned me out,

her two-faced wrists tied
to my bedpost. Call me
anything but a freak, I've
been called everything but

a child of god, every sin I have
committed has been an act of
self-love, I did what any man
in my own shoes would do.

Gluttony

I got beans, greens, potatoes, tomatoes,
lamb, ham, chicken, duck. You name it.
I know better than to fix a to-go plate.
The takeaway is, there are no leftovers

if we all got a seat at god's table.
Mac and cheese, catfish, cornbread,
so much hot sauce the sunset drips.
Big Momma cooks in god's kitchen.

Diabetes means she sits at the right
hand of the father. Lick-your-lips rib tips,
oxtails, grits, gumbo, black-eyed peas,
hoecakes, and sweet potato pie.

Any grandma worth her salt has worn
out her knees in prayer, in hopes that
scraps be nourishment to our bodies.
Do you know what it is to go without?

Greed

When I first met god
he owned me. I had dollar bills
tucked behind each ear.
At great cost, he taught me

love of money is a weapon,
the color green suggestive
in its very nature.
Women lie. Men lie.

Numbers don't lie.
None of my shit
is in god's name
but the light bill.

Is it shame on me
or shame on you
for wanting what
we can't afford?

Anger

I've been acting up since
I left my daddy's nuts.
So what I gotta attitude?
I'm big mad for no rhyme

or reason. It's lemon pepper
season, chickens coming home
to roost. I make St. Louis feel
its ears ring. I'm Apollo Creed,

heavyweight world champ.
I don't suffer no fools.
I don't shit where I eat.
You a cheat so I flipped

the spades table fifty-'leven feet.
Back, back, back, back.
I made my hand into a gun
and I hit you with the heat.

Heresy

Raised a Catholic,
I have wondered whether
god exists. Before god could
get his hands on me, the world

left me burned. Black Galileo,
I rode the earth around the sun.
Whether flat or round, I engage
in foreplay. Love me or curse me,

just let my soul be.
Word is bond. That part.
What's today's mathematics?
Down for the count,

I pledged allegiance to whatever
mumbo jumbo I was fed.
The fool is full of certainty,
the wise man full of doubt.

Violence

One, two, three, it's kind
of dangerous to be in poetry.
I shot Death and the horse she
rode in on. Murder was the case

that they gave me. In my casket
I had a razor in each cheek.
Stay ready so you don't have to get ready.
Wanna bumble with the bee?

I'll throw a hex on your whole family.
A lesson on craft from *The Craft:*
I put Nair in the shampoo of
Becky with the good hair.

I'll split your wig if you don't
put some respect on my name.
I make a tiger look tame.
Ghostface Killah, a threat I remain.

Fraud

Fake it till you make it. Save face.
I'm the BBL, bigmouth aunty
with faux grace and knockoff style,
hocus-pocus, Coke-bottle figure,

red onion bogus, enough tears
in my eyes to fake the funk.
Before the final buzzard
of deliverance,

I made myself into a god.
My pump fake made ballers
call me a false prophet.
Fool you once, shame on me;

fool you twice, shame on you.
Show me a woman without a hustle
and I'll find you a man
to play dead.

Treachery

Any and all smack talk,
I'm naughty by nature.
A femme fatale to look out for,
I could be subject to change.

Fortune and women cheat, trick, deceive.
Both are inconstant and unstable,
but when my turntables
get wobbly they don't fall.

It's a cold day in hell when
an army of ants plays with fire.
Sometimes everything goes
wrong for the right reason.

If this reaches you, godspeed.
Leave heaven's back door cracked.
Eyes closed, wide shut,
I will feel my way there.

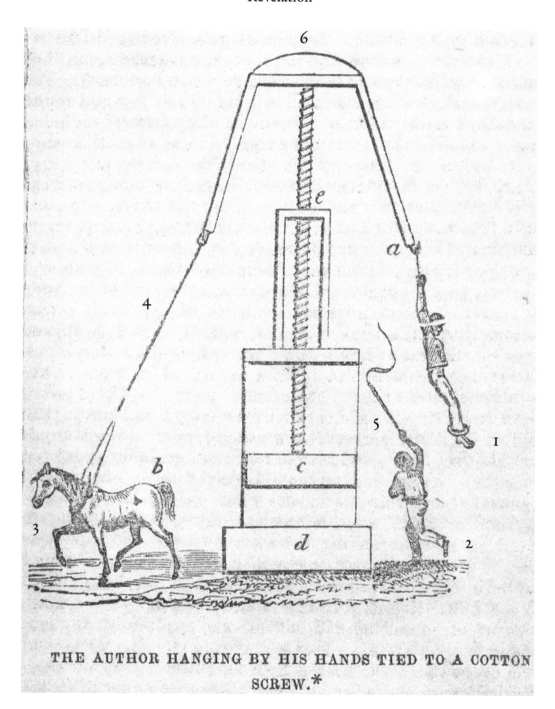

THE AUTHOR HANGING BY HIS HANDS TIED TO A COTTON
SCREW.*

A. AUTHOR AS ANGEL

    1. *And I saw another mighty angel come down from heaven, clothed with a cloud: and a rainbow was upon his head, and his face was as it were the sun, and his feet as pillars of fire:*

    2. *And he had in his hand a little book open: and he set his right foot upon the sea, and his left foot on the earth,*

B. AUTHOR AS ANIMAL

    3. *And cried with a loud voice, as when a lion roareth: and when he had cried, seven thunders uttered their voices.*

C. MYSTERY AS MACHINE

    4. *And when the seven thunders had uttered their voices, I was about to write: and I heard a voice from heaven saying unto me, Seal up those things which the seven thunders uttered, and write them not.*

D. SEALED BOX

    5. *And the angel which I saw stand upon the sea and upon the earth lifted up his hand to heaven,*

E. MYSTERY AS MASTERY

    6. *And sware by him that liveth for ever and ever, who created heaven, and the things that therein are, and the earth, and the things that therein are, and the sea, and the things which are therein, that there should be time no longer.*

Quartet for the End of Time

for Olivier Messiaen

I

If you play me, then you
play yourself. That was
all the dead needed

to say. To get the better
of time, we got better
with time. I left my body

and took on the look
of a man. I made him
an honest woman.

A diagram of this
sentence builds a
structure made from

wind. Inside that
house is a box. Inside
the box is the head

of a goat. Inside the
goat: a knife's quiet
song. The blade of

desire is the silver in
my teeth. My mouth
has a certain ring to it.

II

I will take you now to after-
life's kitchen, where the salty
girls cure meat with their tears.

Only through time is time
conquered. Come correct.
Come prepared to sit at the table

of contents. We bow our heads,
count our blessings like
little pigs, while the king-

fisher waits for a shaft of
sun. *Sprint,* said the bird,
for the foothills of truth.

Stop, stop, stop, said the bird,
there is mischief afoot. Then
we sat and ate with our hands

an entire field of wild thyme.
When asked to choose a hill
to die on, we wanted to kill

the bird. To reconcile our pain
we made the stars into a bear.
Myth made all the difference.

III

If your wrist holds a five-
nailed star, clock the T.
Who can open the door to night

and not see themselves in black?
Not I. For thousands of years,
I have sat on a milk crate.

Stationed at the crossroads, I sing:
Bone, bone, bone, bone, bone.
I don a yellow jacket and fox-

gloves to push out the sun.
The morning is such a production.
A ghost—aghast at the sound

of singe, a crowned knot of fire.
There is no sense to be had
in the country of our making.

This language a garden
of strain. No limit
soldiers, we marched

to the drum of empty
cups, and if a spoon fell
a woman was cursed.

IV

When I was sold
down the river,
god set down his book

in the shape of a tent.
That day I was born again—
my limbs, American letters.

The stairway to heaven is
yellow-boned legs, antiqued
in their quadroon rust.

At the gate to eternity,
a lawn jockey grins wide
as the science of mercy.

In his hands a badminton
racket. He swats and we
see how they run, how

crickets gallop in the
dark like horseflies.
Heaven is a thousand

chandeliers, every crystal
a single body, each head
a grizzly sparkle.

Beware of the End Word

for Marvin Tate

newsroom   nasty   *Never, never again!*

Neptune   Nantucket   Nairobi

no-count   non sequiturs   *She said, "NO!"*

9 feet under   noisy   N[   ]   nearsighted

Nastradamus   nickel bag

nylons   neckties   noose

necromancy   nary   nothing   napki

Knuck if you buck!   Nubian   Negro   newborn

nil   nominal   narcolepsy

newfangled   not   nirva

Naw!   null   noun   nude   nipple   neighborho

9 ½ years   needy   nutcrac

neuter   numerator   nuclear   neutron

naysayer   nadir   normal   numb

neon   Nike   neroli   notice   *There a*

nonstop   nail   naughty

nonfiction   Nino   1999

Nicaragua   Newark   Nigeria

    Negroni   nightgown   9:30 p.m.   nunchucks

    Nay Nay   neurosis   natural

nukes   nappy   nut sack   never mind

          nix   no luck   nicknack

    nevertheless   nougat   nose hairs

          named   nationalist   Nathaniel

Na na na na boo boo!   nimble   Nia

    nomenclature   notebook   nowhere

atch   no-good   never-never land

    Not today!   Nixon   *nihilist*   nonsense

neither   nanometer   *Now and Later*

nugget   *Nope!*   negative   *Beware of the N word!*

ace program for niggas!   'nem   North

          narcotic   neutral   number runner

Steal Away

Time takes off its yellowed
dust jacket, decides to stay
awhile. It is raining out-
side, but just because
water is in a rush
does not mean that
time must be. Naked,
in a splash of sunlight,
wreathed in a cloud's
white envelope, follow
the letter of the law: *I*—
it leads the little engine
that could be called
a body. Behind every
machine is a timer of
some sort, sorting the
rocks from the beans,
kidneys' light work.

*

Time takes off with kinetic
kinfolk in tow, like a bat
out of hell, heartbroken,
wing muscle caught in
the thorny rain. Reminds
me of that scene in
The Five Heartbeats.
When a character is given
an animal nickname like
"Duck," what does it mean?
For example, when you

duck down from danger,
are you more human or
animal? The body sheds
rain we call sweat.
Undressed, unlawful,
time loses itself, lost in
the machinery of men.

*

Time takes off, belated
minutiae. It's the little
things, the subtle details
that take on a life of their
own. When faced with
the clock beating its chest
with scissored hands,
disengage, look away.
Rain, rain, go away,
come again another day
with a tree-sap glue stick
and the fallen leaves of
colorful cardiac arrest.
The Steel Yard is an iron
garden in bloom, perfumed
weapons of mass erection.
The scent is like a trail
of breaded wood chips.

*

Time takes off patent
leather shoes, one at a

time. Lace socks follow.
Inside every piano is a harp.
Delicate fuzz between toes.
Time is a window, a door,
a mirror of meteorology.
Law abides by weather's
predictions, nine times out
of ten snow days. Apart
from my intellectual
property, how do I legally
become a part of the
institution without
becoming institutionalized?
A nonrobot in robotics
club, checking the box
for *I am not a robot.*

With the Future behind Us

after Aymara language

We can't see the future,
therefore, it is behind us.

The past is known,
hence, it lies ahead.

The present is peripheral vision,
we try to make predictions

in any given moment, we can't
tell up from down, right from

the wrong that goes left.
God places us on standby.

The hairs have eyes in
our backward heads, for

the future is at our backs.
The past—right in front of us.

Black Bell

A bell's dome represents the whole universe, the flat bottom represents the earth, and the hollow inside represents the space between the rest of the universe and the earth. When you strike a bell it sends a message from Earth out into the universe. Before reading, strike a bell tuned to A, the note connected to the third-eye chakra.

Wore the whistles
of men down her back.

Her clapper hung
like a saggy breast,
a piece of music.

Beneath her skirt was
the truth made ugly. Unsweet
as blackberry thorns.

Her laughter's rattle, a mask
for secret contempt.
She took in as much

as she could. A homely,
or rather timely,
air about her.

Inside the wall of her cheek
was a sliver of violence
only she could trust.

The wind would witness
but wouldn't chime in.

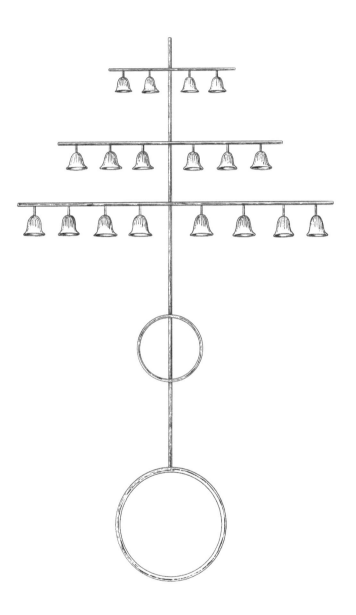

Notes

"A Bell Is a Messenger of Time" riffs on Arthur Jafa's *Love Is The Message, The Message Is Death.*

"The Art of Dancing Explained by Reading Female Figures" includes an 1837 illustration from the London publication of Moses Roper's *A Narrative of the Adventures and Escape of Moses Roper, from American Slavery* located in the Schomburg Center for Research in Black Culture—Manuscripts, Archives and Rare Books Division, titled *A Woman with Iron Horns and Bells On.* The poem also includes a plate from Kellom Tomlinson's 1735 publication *The Art of Dancing Explained by Reading and Figures.*

"Black Bell" is a series of four poems, one in each section of the collection, written in tribute to the woman featured in the archival illustration *A Woman with Iron Horns and Bells On.* This series is designed to send messages, as one makes their way through the book, from the earth out into the universe. I encourage the reader to reflect on all their encounters in the world with bells, including the one that hangs in a tree on the McLeod Plantation Historic Site in Charleston, South Carolina. I also invite the reader to consider this 1977 quote from *The Combahee River Collective Statement:* "If Black women were free, it would mean that everyone else would have to be free since our freedom would necessitate the destruction of all the systems of oppression."

"The Respiratory System" is in conversation with the knowledge that Phillis Wheatley suffered from chronic asthma and tuberculosis. The poem borrows a line from Thalia Field's "HI ADAM!" in *Personhood* and the title of Theaster Gates's Serpentine Pavilion 2022 *Black Chapel.*

"Phillis Wheatley Takes Turing Test" was written with a debt to Franny Choi's poem "Turing Test," from her collection *Soft Science.* Some of the poem's lines are adapted from Antonio Porchia's *Voices,* translated by W.S. Merwin; from the last stanza of Margaret Atwood's "Variation on the Word Sleep," from *Selected Poems II: Poems Selected and New, 1976–1986;* and from the *Online Etymology Dictionary* (etymonline.com). Other sources of inspiration were Henry Louis Gates Jr.'s article "Phillis Wheatley on Trial," in the 20 January 2003 issue of *The New Yorker,* and "The Poem That Passed the Turing Test" by Brian Merchant, published 5 February 2015 in *VICE.*

"The Loophole of Retreat, or The Love below, as Above" is written in regard to Harriet Jacobs's 1861 *Incidents in the Life of a Slave Girl,* where she writes of her confinement in a garret: "I lived in that little dismal hole, almost deprived of light and air, and with no space to move my limbs, for nearly seven years. . . . My body still suffers from the effects of that long imprisonment, to say nothing of my soul."

"Space Is the Place" takes its title from the Sun Ra song, on the album *The Other Side of the Sun.*

"Hymn of Inscape" takes inspiration from sources including the historical figures Henry "Box" Brown, Lear Green, and Harriet Jacobs, as well as Monica Youn's poem "Detail of the Rice Chest," in *From From;* Dawn Lundy Martin's *Life in a Box Is a Pretty Life;* Gerard Manley Hopkins's concept of "inscape"; and the sentence "We build our temples for tomorrow, strong as we know how, and we stand on top of the mountain, free within ourselves," in Langston Hughes's essay "The Negro Artist and the Racial Mountain," from *The Collected Works of Langston Hughes: Essays on Art, Race, Politics, and World Affairs.* The poem's use of columns is at play with Jacques Derrida's *Glas,* translated to *Clang,* which is formatted with parallel texts discussing G.W.F. Hegel and Jean Genet.

"The Presence of the Body" uses a diagram illustrating the "stage or dancing room" in Raoul-Auger Feuillet's *Orchesography; or, The Art of Dancing by Characters and Demonstrative Figures* (1715), translated from the French by John Weaver, and an 1872 engraving on paper found in the National Portrait Gallery of the Smithsonian Institution titled *Lear Green Escaping in a Chest.*

"Unbelievable Time Required to Cover Immense Distances of Love" is taken from an illustration found in the rare books holdings of Colorado College's Special Collections at the Charles L. Tutt Library.

"Love in Outer Space" takes its title from the Sun Ra song, on the album *Purple Night.*

"[American Journal]" takes its title from Robert Hayden's poem "[American Journal]," in the collection *American Journal.* The poem samples phrases from Martín Espada's *Imagine the Angels of Bread* and Samuel R. Delany's *Stars in My Pocket Like Grains of Sand.* The closing lines are adapted from Ilya Kaminsky's *Deaf Republic.*

"Door of the Cosmos" takes its title from the Sun Ra song, on the album *Sleeping Beauty.*

"Springtime Again" takes its title from the Sun Ra song, on the album *Sleeping Beauty,* and is also inspired by Danez Smith's "summer, somewhere," from *Don't Call Us Dead.* The poem references Ne-Yo's song "Mirror," Master P's "Make 'em Say Ugh," and the Wu-Tang Clan's "C.R.E.A.M."

"Over the Rainbow" takes its title from the Sun Ra song, on the album *Somewhere Over the Rainbow,* and is deeply influenced by Taylor Johnson's poem "This is a review for Blue in Green by Miles Davis," from *Inheritance.*

"Bridge between Starshine and Clay" takes its title from lines in Lucille Clifton's poem "won't you celebrate with me," from *The Book of Light.*

"Time with Stevie Wonder in It" takes its title from Christopher Gilbert's poem, in *Across the Mutual Landscape.* My poem functions as an ekphrasis of a photograph of Teddy Pendergrass.

"The Clearing" takes its title from JJJJJerome Ellis's album and book *The Clearing.* The line "MUSICK is a clock of Snow" comes from one of Ellis's online readings of his poetry. The poem also utilizes an iconic phrase from Vogue Ballroom's MC Debra.

"Climate Crisis Could Kill Off Great Tits, Scientists Warn" takes its title from a circulating X (formerly Twitter) tagline in relation to a 12 November 2020 *Independent* article titled "Earlier springs could cause common bird species to become extinct by end of the century, scientists warn."

"A Song by Any Other Name" contains a quote from Thomas Jefferson's *Notes on the State of Virginia.*

"A Gentle Dialogue between Eternity and the Hours" borrows a line from *Malcolm X,* directed by Spike Lee.

"Garden of the Gods" takes its name from the registered National Natural Landmark. The poem is inspired by the sandstone rock formations in Colorado Springs, Colorado.

"Hymn of Thanksgiving" utilizes a broadside from about 1849, found in the John Hay Library's Harris Collection of American Poetry and Plays at Brown University.

"Elegy for Dred Scott" is in conversation with the Dred Scott decision, formally *Dred Scott v. John F.A. Sandford,* the legal case in which the US Supreme Court, on 6 March

1857, ruled (7–2) that a slave (Dred Scott) who had resided in a free state and territory (where slavery was prohibited) was not thereby entitled to his freedom; that African Americans were not and could never be citizens of the United States; and that the Missouri Compromise (1820), which had declared free all territories west of Missouri and north of latitude 36°30', was unconstitutional.

"St. Louis Blues" is named after the popular American blues song composed by W.C. Handy. The poem borrows language from the OutKast song "Skew It on the Bar-B," from the album *Aquemini,* and adapts a line from the film *The Last Black Man in San Francisco.*

"A Bell Is a Bearer of Time" utilizes a sentence from Hortense J. Spillers's "Moving on Down the Line," published in the March 1988 *American Quarterly,* and from Saidiya V. Hartman's "Venus in Two Acts," published in *Small Axe* in 2008. My poem also contains an altered line from Hilton Als's *The Women* and a phrase I heard the poet Tyrone Williams say in a craft talk at Pacific Northwest College of Art.

"Idiophone, or Memory Is a Strange Bell" uses a form inspired by sam sax's poem "A Very Small Animal Entirely Surrounded by Water" and lyrics from Erykah Badu's song "Telephone," on the album *New Amerykah Part One (4th World War).* The title "Memory Is a Strange Bell" is borrowed from an Emily Dickinson line and from the Ogden Museum of Southern Art's exhibition *Memory Is a Strange Bell: The Art of William Christenberry.*

"Letter from the End of the World" takes its title and first line from Lisel Mueller's poem, in *The Private Life.*

"A Child Is like a Clarinet" is dedicated to Eliza Harris, who escaped enslavement by crossing the freezing Ohio River, negotiating pieces of breaking ice while holding her baby, and to Henri Akoka, an Algerian Jewish clarinetist who escaped a World War II German prisoner-of-war truck by "jumping onto the top of a moving train with his clarinet under his arm." Akoka, while held by Nazi forces, was part of the original quartet who performed Olivier Messiaen's *Quatuor pour la fin du temps.*

"The Budding Soul" takes its title from poet Cécile Sauvage's collection *L'Âme en bourgeon.* Sauvage was the mother of Olivier Messiaen.

"John Cage Meets Sun Ra" takes its title from the album *John Cage Meets Sun Ra.* The last stanza is a variation on the last line of Rita Dove's poem "Canary," from *Grace Notes.*

"For Henry 'Box' Brown, from Alison 'Inbox' @ Brown" borrows lines from RaMell Ross's website (ramellross.com).

"Got 'til It's Gone" is indebted, for its visual accompaniments of "runaway ads," to Freedom on the Move, a database of fugitives from North American slavery. The poem takes its title and borrows some lyrics from the song by Janet Jackson, featuring Q-Tip and Joni Mitchell, on Jackson's album *The Velvet Rope*.

"Cognitive Mapping" was originally written for a reading with Lyn Hejinian for the 100 Boots Poetry Series at Pulitzer Arts in St. Louis, Missouri.

"We Gave the Clock a Face" takes its title from Lisel Mueller's "Things," from *Alive Together: New and Selected Poems*, and draws inspiration from Paul Tran's "Galileo," in *All the Flowers Kneeling*.

"Swing Low, Sweet Chariot" remixes and weaves Emily Dickinson's "Because I could not stop for Death," Sonia Sanchez's *Does Your House Have Lions?*, T.S. Eliot's "The Waste Land," and Phillis Wheatley's "On Being Brought from Africa to America."

"The Body Keeps the Musical Score" uses an 1852 wood engraving found in the Miriam and Ira D. Wallach Division of Art, Prints and Photographs: Picture Collection, the New York Public Library. The wood engraver is Jas. Wilson & Son. The poem title draws on Bessel van der Kolk's *The Body Keeps the Score: Brain, Mind, and Body in the Healing of Trauma*.

"A Recipe for the Common Task" is dedicated to Nikolai Fyodorovich Fyodorov (1829–1903), a Russian teacher, librarian, and philosopher who is credited with starting the Russian cosmism movement, a precursor of transhumanism. He conceptualized "radical life extension, physical immortality, and resurrection of the dead" as "The Common Task" or duty of Christians, thereby making science on par with art and religion.

"The Body Faceup" uses a diagram illustrating the "face or fore part of the body up" in Raoul-Auger Feuillet's *Orchesography; or, The Art of Dancing by Characters and Demonstrative Figures* (1715), translated from the French by John Weaver. The poem also uses *The resurrection of Henry Box Brown at Philadelphia, Who escaped from Richmond VA. in a box 3 feet long 2½ ft. deep and 2 ft. wide,* an 1850 image found in the Library of Congress Prints and Photographs Division.

"Regeneration" is a remix of Suji Kwock Kim's poem "Generation," which opens *Notes from the Divided Country.* The phrase and concept of *landless acknowledgments* is borrowed from Nate Marshall's poem "landless acknowledgment," in *Finna.*

"True and False Characters" pairs a diagram labeled "From the 3rd true to the 1st false" in "A table of the changing true positions into false positions" from Raoul-Auger Feuillet's *Orchesography; or, The Art of Dancing by Characters and Demonstrative Figures* (1715), translated from the French by John Weaver, with the illustration *A Woman with Iron Horns and Bells On* from *A Narrative of the Adventures and Escape of Moses Roper, from American Slavery* (1837).

"Change of Positions" employs a plate from Kellom Tomlinson's 1735 publication *The Art of Dancing Explained by Reading and Figures,* as well as "Ellen Craft, the fugitive slave," the frontispiece image from the 1860 publication *Running a Thousand Miles for Freedom; or, The Escape of William and Ellen Craft from Slavery.*

"But for the Love of God" borrows a refrain from the Nicki Minaj and Beyoncé song "Feeling Myself," from Nicki Minaj's album *The Pinkprint.*

"Nine Circles of Hell (36 Chambers)" is in conversation with the nine concentric circles of Hell as described in Dante's *Inferno,* the first part of the *Divine Comedy.* Overall, the poem is in dialogue with the Wu-Tang Clan's album *Enter the Wu-Tang (36 Chambers).* The poem remixes many hip-hop songs including Yo Gotti's "Women Lie, Men Lie," featuring Lil Wayne, Leikeli47's "Attitude," Lil' O's "Back Back," Black Star's "Definition," OutKast's "Aquemini," Puff Daddy's "It's All About the Benjamins," and "Beans Greens Potatoes Tomatoes" (a remix of the gospel singer Shirley Caesar).

"Revelation" utilizes an illustration found in Moses Roper's *A Narrative of the Adventures and Escape of Moses Roper, from American Slavery* (1837), as well as scripture from the Bible (King James Version), Revelation 10:1–6. Revelation 10 also served as inspiration for Olivier Messiaen's *Quatuor pour la fin du temps.*

"Quartet for the End of Time" is inspired, in part, by Olivier Messiaen's composition *Quatuor pour la fin du temps,* which was written while Messiaen was a prisoner of war in Germany and premiered in 1941, as performed by fellow prisoners. The poem is also in conversation with Nick Cave's exhibition *Until* and T.S. Eliot's *Four Quartets,* and it opens with a riff on the chorus from Beyoncé's "Don't Hurt Yourself," featuring Jack White, on the album *Lemonade.*

"Beware of the End Word" borrows lines from Marvin Tate's songs "N-Word (Part 1)" and "N-Word (Part 2)," on the album *Marvin Tate's D-Settlement,* as well as a refrain from A Tribe Called Quest's song "The Space Program," on the album *We Got It from Here . . . Thank You 4 Your Service;* from Nas's "Nastradamus," on the album *Nastradamus;* and from Crime Mob's "Knuck if You Buck," featuring Lil Scrappy, on the album *Crime Mob.* The form of various poems in Tyehimba Jess's *Olio* also served as inspiration for this poem.

Acknowledgments

Thank you to the editors of the journals in which many of the poems in this book appeared, often in different versions and/or earlier forms:

The Academy of American Poets Poem-a-Day: "Love in Outer Space"

The Adroit Journal: "A Song by Any Other Name"

The American Poetry Review: "Garden of the Gods," "Letter from the End of the World," "Phillis Wheatley Takes Turing Test," and "Springtime Again"

Indiana Review: "The Clearing," "Idiophone, or Memory Is a Strange Bell," "Live Long and Prosper," and "The Respiratory System"

The Massachusetts Review: "A Bell Is a Messenger of Time" and "Steal Away"

Meridian: "Cognitive Mapping"

Poetry: "A Bell Is a Bearer of Time," "The Loophole of Retreat, or The Love below, as Above," "Quartet for the End of Time," and "What the Lyric Be"

Revolute: "Beware of the End Word" and "Black Bell" (Wore the whistles)

The Rumpus: "But for the Love of God," "Look back at It," and "Swing Low, Sweet Chariot"

Tupelo Quarterly: "[American Journal]"

Many Thanks . . .

Sincere thanks to the voices of the archive, both silent and singing, and the librarians as well as archivists who tend to the dead; to all the black bells across time and space; to those who make noise, music, sound, poetry, in whatever forms they can.

To my husband, Nate Marshall: "you are the perfect verse over a tight beat." Thank you for paying to print out my manuscript at the University of Wisconsin–Madison library and for the first time giving me the experience of laying out the pages across the living room floor.

For my womb, which became a bell, and my daughter's heart beating inside me as I completed this book.

To Paul Tran, my sister, thank you for helping to edit some of these poems in the Wildflower restaurant in the Central West End of St. Louis.

To my family—grandparents, mother, father, and two sisters.

For friendship in words and life: Fatimah Asghar, Cameron Awkward-Rich, Franny Choi, Safia Elhillo, Eve L. Ewing, Chris Gabo, Airea D. Matthews, Hieu Minh Nguyen, José Olivarez, sam sax, and Danez Smith.

The Copper Canyon team, with special thanks to Michael Wiegers for championing and giving my work a home, as well as Ashley E. Wynter, Ryo Yamaguchi, and Janeen Armstrong.

To those whose paths I crossed at Brown University, especially Thalia Field, Avery Willis Hoffman, Erica Hunt, Tracie Morris, Sawako Nakayasu, Kevin Quashie, and my thesis advisor, Matthew Shenoda. Gratitude also to Nicole Sealey for looking at the first drafts of the "Black Bell" series during her time as writer in residence.

To the Steel Yard and Binch Press/Queer.Archive.Work for offering me artist community in Providence and for the opportunity to expand my imagination both on and off the page.

To Adam Busch and Lisa Yun Lee for the gift of a home away from home in every sense.

To the Harvard Radcliffe Institute Fellowship Program and to the Brown Arts Institute for the David Dornstein '85 Artist Grant as well as a research fellowship, which allowed me to travel to London to support Theaster Gates's exhibition *Black Chapel,* which featured next to its entrance a bell salvaged from St. Laurence, a landmark Catholic church that once stood in Chicago's South Side.

To all the places and forums where I have read/performed this work as it was in process, including Cave Canem, the Cathedral of Learning at the University of Pittsburgh, the Poetry Foundation, Elliott Bay Book Company, and the Rigamarole "poetry house show" at Cam and Franny's.

About the Author

Alison C. Rollins (born and raised in St. Louis) holds a bachelor of science in psychology from Howard University, a master of library and information science from the University of Illinois Urbana-Champaign, and a master of fine arts from Brown University. In 2019, she was named a National Endowment for the Arts literature fellow. Her work, across genres, has appeared in *The American Poetry Review, The Iowa Review, The New York Times Magazine,* and elsewhere. A Cave Canem and Callaloo fellow, she was a 2016 recipient of the Poetry Foundation's Ruth Lilly and Dorothy Sargent Rosenberg Fellowship. Rollins has been awarded support from Harvard University's Radcliffe Institute, the Brown Arts Institute, and the Bread Loaf Writers' Conference. She received the 2018 Rona Jaffe Foundation Writers' Award and a 2020 Pushcart Prize, and her debut poetry collection, *Library of Small Catastrophes* (Copper Canyon Press, 2019), was a 2020 Hurston/Wright Foundation Legacy Award nominee. Rollins has held faculty as well as librarian appointments at institutions including the School of the Art Institute of Chicago, Colorado College, and Pacific Northwest College of Art. She is an assistant professor of English at the University of Wisconsin–Madison.

Copper Canyon Press is deeply grateful to the following individuals whose philanthropic vision and love of poetry made *Black Bell* possible.

Shawn and Lynne Aebi

Zeinab Masud Agha

Loretta Atkins and Martha Trolin

John Bennett

Twanna P. Bolling

David Brewster and Mary Kay Sneeringer

Adam Bush and Lisa Yun Lee

Harriett M. Cody and Harvey Sadis

Linda Corbett

Clyde E. Daniels

Pierce E. Davis

In honor of Catherine Harris

Christin Jaye

Bruce Kelley

In honor of Randall Lane

M. Carol Leber

Elizabeth Douglas Mornin

Walter Parsons

Kevin Prufer

Delphi Psmith

Ella Raymond

Susan Bibi Rollins

Avery Canada Rollins Marshall

Ira Silverberg

Rick Simonson

Chrissy Stegman

Kaci X. Tavares

Jie Tian

Margaret H. Wagner

Poetry is vital to language and living. Since 1972, Copper Canyon Press has published extraordinary poetry from around the world to engage the imaginations and intellects of readers, writers, booksellers, librarians, teachers, students, and donors.

WE ARE GRATEFUL FOR THE MAJOR SUPPORT PROVIDED BY:

academy of
american poets

OFFICE OF ARTS & CULTURE

SEATTLE

amazon *literary partnership*

THE PAUL G. ALLEN
FAMILY FOUNDATION

CULTURE

POETRY

FOUNDATION

Hawthornden
Foundation

INGRAM
CONTENT GROUP

the point
envision · enact · evolve

Lannan

WASHINGTON STATE
ARTS COMMISSION

National
Endowment
for the Arts
arts.gov

ART WORKS.

The Witter Bynner Foundation
for Poetry

TO LEARN MORE ABOUT UNDERWRITING
COPPER CANYON PRESS TITLES,
PLEASE CALL 360-385-4925 EXT. 103

WE ARE GRATEFUL FOR THE MAJOR SUPPORT PROVIDED BY:

Anonymous

Richard Andrews and
  Colleen Chartier

Jill Baker and Jeffrey Bishop

Anne and Geoffrey Barker

Donna Bellew

Will Blythe

John Branch

Diana Broze

John R. Cahill

Sarah Cavanaugh

Keith Cowan and Linda Walsh

Stephanie Ellis-Smith and
  Douglas Smith

Mimi Gardner Gates

Gull Industries Inc.
  on behalf of William True

Carolyn and Robert Hedin

David and Jane Hibbard

Bruce S. Kahn

Phil Kovacevich and Eric Wechsler

Maureen Lee and Mark Busto

Ellie Mathews and Carl Youngmann
  as The North Press

Larry Mawby and Lois Bahle

Petunia Charitable Fund and
  adviser Elizabeth Hebert

Suzanne Rapp and Mark Hamilton

Adam and Lynn Rauch

Emily and Dan Raymond

Joseph C. Roberts

Cynthia Sears

Kim and Jeff Seely

Tree Swenson

Barbara and Charles Wright

In honor of C.D. Wright,
  from Forrest Gander

Caleb Young as C. Young Creative

The dedicated interns and faithful
  volunteers of Copper Canyon Press

The pressmark for Copper Canyon Press
suggests entrance, connection, and interaction
while holding at its center
an attentive, dynamic space for poetry.

This book is set in Garamond Premier Pro.
Book design by Phil Kovacevich.
Printed on archival-quality paper.